STORYBOOK
DOllS to knit

LEISURE ARTS, INC.
Little Rock, Arkansas

EDITORIAL STAFF
Editor-in-Chief: Susan White Sullivan
Director of Designer Relations: Cheryl Johnson
Special Projects Director: Susan Frantz Wiles
Senior Prepress Director: Mark Hawkins
Art Publications Director: Rhonda Shelby
Technical Writer: Sarah J. Green
Technical Editor: Lindsay Diane White
Editorial Writer: Susan McManus Johnson
Art Category Manager: Lora Puls
Senior Publications Designer: Dana Vaughn
Graphic Artist: Becca Snider
Imaging Technician: Stephanie Johnson
Photography Manager: Katherine Laughlin
Contributing Photographer: Ken West
Contributing Photostylist: Sondra Daniel
Publishing Systems Administrator: Becky Riddle
Mac Information Technology Specialist:
    Robert Young

BUSINESS STAFF
President and Chief Executive Officer: Rick Barton
Vice President and Chief Operations Officer:
    Tom Siebenmorgen
Vice President of Sales: Mike Behar
Director of Finance and Administration:
    Laticia Mull Dittrich
National Sales Director: Martha Adams
Creative Services: Chaska Lucas
Information Technology Director: Hermine Linz
Controller: Francis Caple
Vice President, Operations: Jim Dittrich
Retail Customer Service Manager: Stan Raynor
Print Production Manager: Fred F. Pruss

CD Narrator: Libby Strawn
CD Production: ARCA Studios, Little Rock, AR

ISBN-13: 978-1-60900-099-8

Library of Congress Control Number: 2010941391

TABLE OF CONTENTS

Classic fairytales come to life when children slip the legs of these Walkabout Puppets onto their fingers! Each knitted and felted character is the creation of Anita M. Wheeless. They are based on seven beloved stories and rhymes, which are recorded on the enclosed audio CD. Youngsters can listen to the tales and play along with Goldilocks & the Three Bears, Humpty-Dumpty, Big Bad Wolf & Three Little Pigs, The Gingerbread Man, Hansel & Gretel and the Witch, Little Red Riding Hood and the Wolf, and Mary & Her Little Lamb. The 17 adorable characters are knitted with wool yarn on double-pointed needles, with embellishments added after felting. With these cute puppets and the handy CD, hours and hours of playtime fun await the young and young-at-heart!

MEET ANITA M. WHEELESS

"I taught myself to knit while waiting for my children at a scholastic chess tournament," says Anita M. Wheeless. "I started with scarves and ended up knitting so many that year, I didn't have enough necks to put them on!"

Anita soon realized that what she really wanted to knit were toys. As she says, "Most of the toy patterns I found were knit flat on two needles, then seamed together. I wondered why there weren't any toy patterns that were 'knit-in-the-round,' so I decided to come up with my own.

"I fell in love with the texture of felted fabric and I now design most of my toys to be felted in the washing machine. Since I love the look of vintage children's book illustrations, I made it my goal to achieve a classic 1920s or 1930s look for these little characters."

Anita lives in North Carolina with her husband Randy. Their three children range in age from 22 to 16, and they have a very bossy bearded collie named Maggie.

3

BASIC doll CONSTRUCTION
TIPS & HINTS

Editor's Note: Before you begin to knit any of the Walkabout dolls, we recommend that you take the time to knit and felt a small swatch with each of the wool yarns you intend to use, especially if you are using a different brand of yarn than was used for our models. You may be inclined to skip this step. But, each wool yarn felts differently. Even the same brands in different colors may shrink more or less. For first time felters, complete felting instructions can be found on page 9. Have fun!

Each Doll in this book is knit on double pointed needles in the same way—starting at the Legs and working up. As you are knitting your Doll, refer to these notes and photos if you need a visual aid to help you.

The instructions are written for one set of 5 double pointed needles. There are four different ways that the needles are used to knit these Dolls.

1. Working in rows with 2 needles on the lower Legs and Body; also ears and aprons

2. Working in the round with 4 needles on the upper Legs and the Arms *(Fig. A)*

Fig. A

3. Working in the round with 5 needles on the upper Body *(Fig. B)*

Fig. B

4. Working in the round with 3 needles on the Head with the Arm stitches either resting on 2 stitch holders *(Fig. C)* or on 2 needles *(Fig. D)*

Fig. C

Fig. D

LEGS

Each of the Dolls' Legs begins with one stitch. Increases are made on each row until you divide all the stitches onto 3 needles to begin working in the round. Once the First Leg is completed, you will slip the stitches from the needles onto 3 small stitch holders so that you can work the Second Leg.

Note: If you should have a second set of the same size needles you used for the First Leg, then you can simply set it aside on the needles with the marker still attached. So, if you have the extra needles, skip the next paragraph and go to the Body Joining.

Working around the First Leg counterclockwise *(Fig. E)*, slip all the stitches onto separate stitch holders *(Fig. F)*. Leave the marker around the first stitch to mark the third stitch holder.

Fig. E

Fig. F

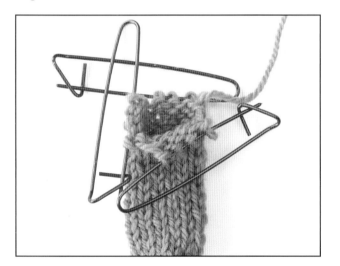

BODY JOINING

The Doll's Body is worked in the same way whether the First Leg is on three stitch holders or on three double pointed needles.

1. With an empty needle, knit across the first needle of the Second Leg and then knit across the first needle or stitch holder of the First Leg *(Fig. G)*, joining the Legs in the front of the Doll.

Fig. G

2. With a second empty needle, work across the second needle or stitch holder on the First Leg.

3. With a third empty needle, knit across the last needle or stitch holder on the First Leg and then knit across the second needle of the Second Leg *(Fig. H)*, joining the Legs in the back of the Doll.

Fig. H

4. Complete the round by using a fourth empty needle to knit across the last needle on the Second Leg. Keep the marker around the first stitch on the Second Leg to mark the beginning of the round and remove the marker from the First Leg.

All the stitches are now divided between 4 needles.

Note: For shaping purposes, at times you will be moving stitches from one needle to the next needle or changing the beginning of the round. The number of stitches on each of the needles is given along with the stitch totals. For example, "8 sts on **each** needle for a total of 24 sts" or "14 sts on first needle, 4 sts on second needle, 14 sts on third needle and 4 sts on fourth needle for a total of 36 sts."

LOWER BODY - BACK OPENING

After joining the Legs, you will be knitting across the stitches on the first needle, then binding off the remaining stitches to leave the back of the Doll open for the "finger pockets."

UPPER BODY SHAPING

The Doll's Upper Body is worked in rows using 2 needles. The first row is an increase row and the second is a dividing row to place the stitches back onto 4 needles to begin working in the round.

Rearranging the stitches onto the 4 needles leaves a partial row to work so that the back of the Doll is joined. Use the last needle to work across these stitches *(Fig. I)*. This places the beginning of the round at the left side. At this point, the first needle is at the left side of the Doll, the second needle is at the front, the third needle is at the right side, and the last needle is at the back.

Fig. J

Fig. I

ARMS

Once the upper Body rounds are complete, increases will be worked in the stitches on the first and third needles to create the Arms. The Arm stitches will be either slipped onto stitch holders *(Fig. C, page 5)* or left on the needles if you are working with 2 sets of needles *(Fig. D, page 5)*.

NECK/HEAD SHAPING

The Neck/Head Shaping is worked in the round with 3 needles, one empty needle and 2 needles with stitches. The two needles are parallel to each other and you simply work across each one.

PICKING UP STITCHES

To pick up a stitch, insert the point of the empty needle under one strand at the Neck edge of the Arm opening *(Fig. J)* or under one strand of stitches on a round where indicated *(Fig. K)* for a Skirt, Apron, or a Boot Tip. When all of the stitches are picked up, the working yarn is joined.

Fig. K

FELTING

Felting is a process that has been around for many years that uses hot water and agitation to transform a knitted piece to a firm, durable fabric. Like magic, the stitches will become almost undetectable. Watching as the piece shrinks and the stitches disappear can be a lot of fun!

Check over your Doll to ensure all the loose ends are woven in (a small bit left hanging out is fine, as you can cut this off after felting). Make sure that gaps around the arms, the bottoms of the feet and the area where the legs were joined have been closed. Place the pieces in a zippered lingerie bag or an old pillowcase that you can tie in a knot. While you don't have to use a felting bag, it helps trap any excess wool lint, protecting your washing machine. It also helps keep track of smaller items.

You may want to add either a pair or two of old blue jeans or several tennis balls to help encourage agitation. The more bumping around, the better! Both jeans and tennis balls are recommended because, unlike towels and other articles of clothing, they don't give off lint of their own that could end up (quite unattractively) stuck into your pieces!

Set your washer for a small load with the hottest water on a long cycle with the most agitation. Sprinkle in a little laundry detergent or use a scant ¼ teaspoon or less of liquid laundry detergent or wool wash.

Check the Doll every 5-10 minutes. Be sure to put your fingers in the legholes each time to stretch them as they felt or they will be too small. If your Doll has a skirt, pull the skirt up as you push your fingers down into the leg holes. Try to stretch the legs of the medium and large Dolls up to the knuckles of your hand. Try to stretch the legs of the small Dolls up to the middle knuckles of your fingers. Use the end of a paintbrush or a skewer to open up the arms, the neck and the head so that they do not felt closed. Repeat these same steps in another five minutes or so.

It may take only one cycle to felt the pieces or it may take several to have the stitches melt into each other. Never let the pieces go through the rinse or spin cycles as it can be very difficult to get them to felt any more afterwards. Do set a timer to remind yourself to check about every five minutes. If your piece needs more time in the washer, simply set the cycle to start again. Ears can sometimes take longer to felt properly than the other pieces.

The best way to tell if the piece is finished is that with a lot of stretching and pulling, your fingers will fit into the legs. You certainly don't want them too small, but you also don't want the legs to slip right off.

Once the pieces have all felted together to your liking, rinse them in warm water and squeeze the pieces gently in a towel to remove the excess water.

Now the fun begins. Your Doll is literally like putty in your hands! You will need to pull it and stretch it and stuff it into shape. Whatever shape it's in while it is drying is the shape it will keep once it's dry, so don't wait to start shaping!

Take the end of the paintbrush again (or a kabob skewer) and poke it up into the neck, head and arms. Be sure you reach all the way down into the tips of the hands. All of these spaces need to be opened up so that you can stuff them sufficiently.

Again, put your fingers into the Doll's legs and pull them up and around your fingers. Don't be afraid to pull very hard. For particularly stubborn legs, let them dry with a finger-sized cylinder shape inside; something like a candy thermometer or a fat tube of lipstick will work quite well.

EARS

Shape the ears while still wet and allow them to dry completely. Once all the pieces are dry and the Heads are stuffed, sew the ears on with matching thread as described below or use photos as a guide for placement.

Wolf

Fold the ears in half lengthwise, pressing your finger into the center of each to create an indentation. Coax the tips of the ears into points.

Stitch the ears securely to the top of the head with matching thread. They should be sewn on vertically, with the pointed tip at the top.

Lamb

Round out the edges of the ears, pressing them with your fingers. Fold the ears in half lengthwise.

Stitch them securely to the sides of the head so that they poke out from the head horizontally.

Bear

Press your finger into the center of each ear. Round out the ears, shaping them all around.

Stitch the ears securely to the top of the bear's head, gathering them a little as you stitch.

Pig

Fold the tips down like little flaps.

Stitch the ears to the tops of the head, with the folded part at the top. If the tips don't fold down enough on their own, you can take a tiny stitch with matching thread to hold them down.

STUFFING

Using polyester fiberfill while the Doll is still damp, poke the stuffing way up into the Head, working it upwards to fill out the Head completely. Use small amounts at a time so that the stuffing doesn't form clumps. Round out the Head, shaping it with your hands. Continue to poke and stuff the body of the Doll all the way down until even the tips of the hands are filled. Lightly stuff the chest area. While you want a little stuffing here, you don't want to overstuff, or the body will be too heavy to walk properly.

When the Doll has been completely stuffed and shaped, set it aside on a towel with the other pieces and allow them to dry. This may take several days.

When the Doll is completely dry, you may remove the stuffing and replace it with fresh polyester stuffing if you like, or if you want to use kapok (as it is nice and soft), remove the polyester fiberfill and, using a dust mask so you won't breathe in all the little fibers, re-stuff the piece.

After the final stuffing, securely stitch closed the back of the Doll just above the leg openings to keep the stuffing in place. Check again for any small holes. If there are any, stitch them closed with matching thread. Now you are ready to embroider the features and attach the hair!

EMBROIDERY STITCHES

Embroidering your felted Doll is slightly different from embroidering cloth. Embroidery stitches are usually made by bringing your needle from the wrong side of your fabric through to the right side. You won't always be able to do this on your Doll. Instead, push your needle through from the front in one spot close to the area that you wish to embroider and bring it out where you *want* to begin. Be careful not to pull the floss or the yarn all the way through. Leave a little bit sticking out from where you went into the Doll and later, when you've finished, you can trim it as close to the Doll as possible. Use 6-strand embroidery floss, pearl cotton No. 5 floss or yarn as directed in the project's instructions. If you're not familiar with these stitches, practice them on one of your swatches before you try embroidering your Doll.

The backstitch: This stitch is worked from right to left. Bring the needle up at 1, go down at 2 and come up at 3 *(Fig. L)*.

Fig. L

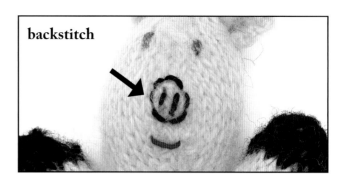

backstitch

The chain stitch: This stitch is worked from right to left. Bring the needle up at 1. Insert your needle down at 1, right next to where you just came up, forming a loop. Keeping the loop below the point of the needle, come up at 2; then go down at 2 to form the second loop *(Fig. M)*. Continue by going back down right next to where you have come up, make another loop, etc.

Fig. M

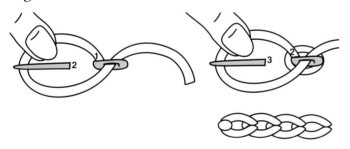

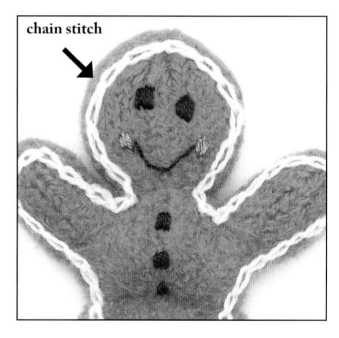

chain stitch

The lazy-daisy stitch: Bring the needle up at 1, then go down again at 1 to form a loop. Come up at 2. Keeping loop below the point of the needle, go down at 3 to anchor loop *(Fig. N)*.

Fig. N

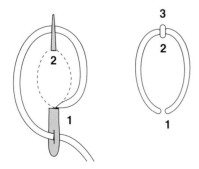

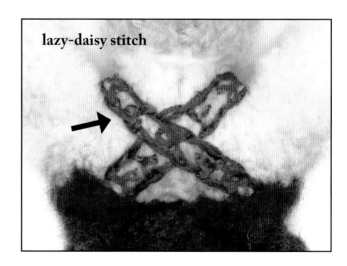

lazy-daisy stitch

The coral stitch: This stitch is worked from right to left. Bring the needle up at 1. Hold the yarn down to the left. Insert the needle down at 2 and come up at 3, making a small vertical stitch across the yarn *(Fig. O)*.

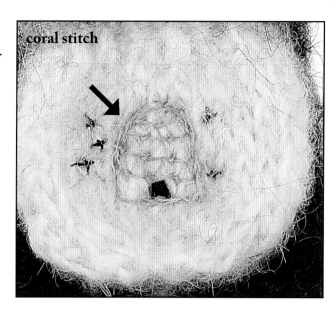
coral stitch

Fig. O

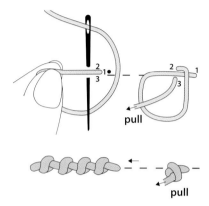

The satin stitch: Bring the needle up at 1, go down at 2, then come up at 3. Continue until area is filled *(Fig. P)*. Work stitches close together, but not overlapping. This is used vertically for the Dolls' eyes and cheeks and the wolves' teeth and horizontally for the wolves' and the bears' noses.

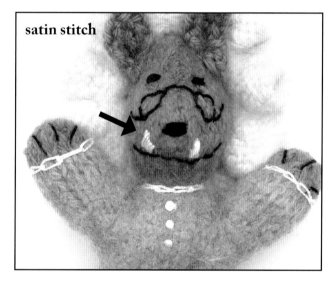
satin stitch

Fig. P

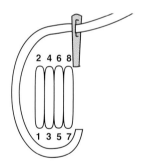

The straight stitch: Straight stitch is just what the name implies, a single, straight stitch. Bring the needle up at 1 and go down at 2 *(Fig. Q)*.

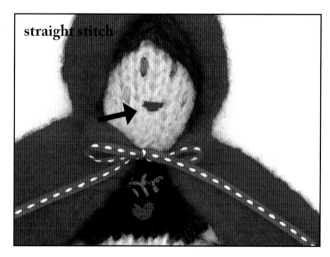
straight stitch

Fig. Q

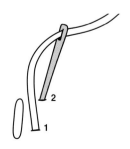

The French knot: Bring needle up at 1. Wrap the yarn around the needle the desired number of times and insert the needle at 2, holding the end of the yarn with the non-stitching fingers *(Fig. R)*. Tighten the knot; then pull the needle through, holding the yarn until it must be released.

Fig. R

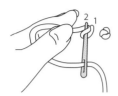

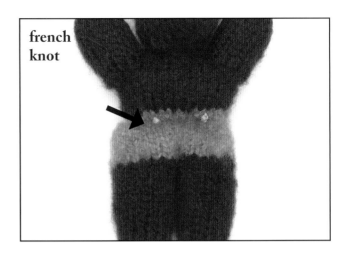

french knot

The scroll stitch: This stitch looks just the like swirly icing on a chocolate-frosted cupcake! Working from left to right, bring your needle up at 1, make a loop of yarn a little to the right. Twist the loop, making sure the yarn coming from your needle is held above the loop. Go down at 2 and up at 3 *(Fig. S)*. When working this stitch for Goldilocks, remember to turn the Doll upside down before you begin.

Fig. S

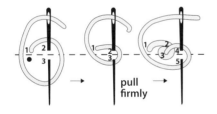

pull firmly

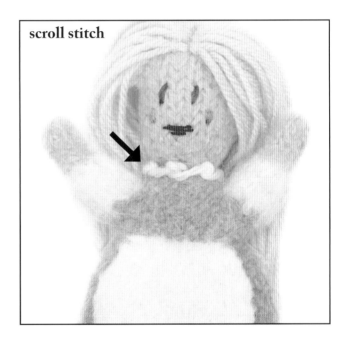

scroll stitch

The split stitch: This stitch is worked from left to right. Bring the needle up at 1 and go down at 2; bring your needle up at 3 in the middle of the previous stitch, splitting the floss or the yarn *(Fig. T)*. Continue in this manner.

Fig. T

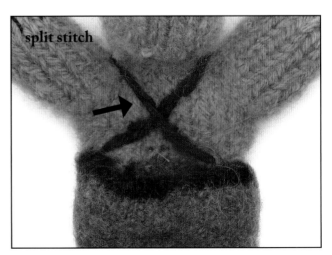

split stitch

The stem stitch: This stitch is worked from left to right. Bring the needle up at 1. Keeping yarn below the stitching line, go down at 2 and come up at 3. Go down at 4 and come up at 5 *(Fig. U)*.

Fig. U

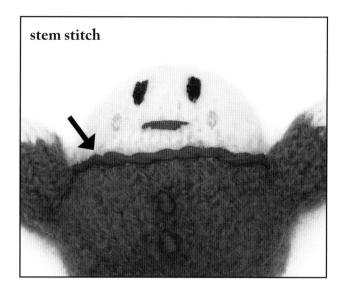

stem stitch

BASIC HAIR

The methods for attaching the hair for the Dolls are very easy! As directed for Hansel, simply make long satin stitches directly onto the Doll's head. When finished, cut the last bit of yarn as close to the head as possible.

For the other Dolls, you'll knot the hair onto the Doll's head just like fringe. Because you'll be folding the hair in half, you'll need to cut the yarn pieces about twice the length you want the finished hair to be.

Be sure to check the placement of the knots as instructed for each Doll.

Working with one strand of yarn at a time, insert the crochet hook in the stitch on the head where you want the strand and pull up a loop with the strand *(Fig. V)*.

Fig. V

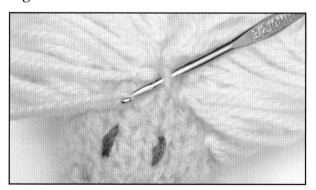

Pull the ends of the strand of yarn through the loop, tightening the knot *(Fig. W)*.

Fig. W

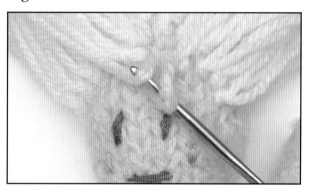

You have one completed knot of hair. Continue knotting the hair as directed for the particular Doll you're making. Once you've worked all the knots, go back and pull on them, making sure they are tight. You can also stitch through the knots into the Doll's head with a bit of matching thread to make sure they are all secure.

GOLDILOCKS and the 3 BEARS

We all know this favorite tale of a little girl who invites herself into the home of three bears while they are away. It is a story that was first told more than two hundred years ago. Back then, it was not a little girl but an old woman who ate the bears' food, sat on their chairs, and slept in their beds. However, both Goldilocks and the old woman learn it isn't nice to help yourself to someone else's belongings.

GOLDILOCKS

■■■□ INTERMEDIATE

Finished Size: Approximately 6½"
(16.5 cm) tall (after felting)

MATERIALS

100% Wool Medium Weight Yarn **[4]**
[3.5 ounces, 220-223 yards
(100 grams, 201-205 meters) per skein]:
Dark Red, Blue, Aran, and Pink -
1 skein **each** color
Double pointed knitting needles,
size 8 (5 mm) - set of 5 needles
Small stitch holders - 3
Split-ring marker
Yarn needle
Tapestry or embroidery needle
Blue, Pink, and Red embroidery floss -
1 skein **each** color
Light Weight Yarn **[3]**
Yellow for hair - small amount
Crochet hook for hair

The model was knit using **Patons® Classic Wool**
#00202 Aran and #77117 Worn Denim, and
Ella Rae Classic #62 Burgundy and #54
Bubblegum. Her hair was made using **Patons®**
Astra #02943 Maize Yellow.

Techniques used:
- Increase *(Figs. 1a & b, page 80)*
- K2 tog *(Fig. 2, page 80)*
- P2 tog tbl *(Fig. 5, page 80)*
- Slip 1, K1, PSSO *(Fig. 6, page 80)*

*Before beginning, read Basic Doll Construction,
pages 4-15.*

FIRST LEG

With Dark Red, cast on one st.

Row 1: (K, P, K) **all** in the same st: 3 sts.

Rows 2 and 3: Increase in each st across: 12 sts.

Row 4: Divide sts onto 3 needles as follows:
K4, (with empty needle, K4) twice: 4 sts on
each of 3 needles.

Place marker around first st and begin working
in rnds *(see Markers, page 79)*.

Rnds 1-3: Knit around; at end of Rnd 3, cut
Dark Red.

Rnds 4-14: With Aran, knit around; at end of
Rnd 14, cut Aran leaving a long end for sewing.

Working counterclockwise, slip sts from each
needle onto 3 separate st holders. Leave marker
to mark third st holder.

SECOND LEG

Work same as First Leg; at end of Rnd 14, do
not cut Aran.

BODY

Joining Rnd: K4 from first needle; with same
needle, K4 from third st holder (front joined),
remove marker; with empty needle, K4 from
second st holder; with empty needle, K4 from
last st holder; with same needle, K4 from next
needle (back joined); with empty needle, knit
last 4 sts: 8 sts on first needle, 4 sts on second
needle, 8 sts on third needle and 4 sts on fourth
needle for a total of 24 sts.

Rnds 1-4: Knit around; at end of Rnd 4, cut Aran.

Rnd 5: With Blue, K8 from first needle; with same needle, K2 from second needle; with empty needle, K2 from second needle; with empty needle, K8 from third needle; with empty needle, K2 from fourth needle; slip last 2 sts from fourth needle onto first needle and remove marker: 12 sts on first needle, 2 sts on second needle, 8 sts on third needle and 2 sts on fourth needle.

Rnd 6: With empty needle, knit 12 sts from first needle; bind off remaining sts, slip last st onto first needle: 13 sts.

Begin working in rows.

Increase Row: K2, increase 11 times: 24 sts.

Dividing Row: Divide sts onto 4 needles as follows: P4 onto **each of** first 2 needles; P8 onto **each of** last 2 needles.

Hold your needles so that they form a square. With **knit** side facing, K4 from last needle onto first needle so that the back is joined. This needle now has 8 sts. With back facing, place marker around first st on left needle that has 4 sts. This is your new first needle.

Next 4 Rnds: Knit around; at end of last rnd, cut Blue.

Increase Rnd: With Aran, increase in each st across first needle, slip sts just worked onto a st holder (Arm), move marker to first st on second needle, cut Aran; with Blue, knit across 8 sts on second needle, drop Blue; with Aran, increase in each st across third needle, slip sts just worked onto a second st holder (Arm), cut Aran; with Blue, knit across 8 sts on last needle: 8 sts on **each** of 2 needles and 8 sts on **each** of 2 st holders for a total of 32 sts.

NECK

Rnds 1 and 2: Knit around: 8 sts on **both** needles for a total of 16 sts.

Rnd 3: K2 tog around: 4 sts on **both** needles for a total of 8 sts.

Rnd 4: Knit around; cut Blue.

HEAD

Rnd 1: With Pink, knit around.

Rnd 2: Increase in each st around: 8 sts on **both** needles for a total of 16 sts.

Rnd 3: (K3, increase, K4) across **each** needle: 9 sts on **both** needles for a total of 18 sts.

Divide sts onto 3 needles as follows: Slip first 3 sts on right hand point of first needle onto an empty needle; slip first 3 sts on left hand point of second needle onto opposite end of same needle: 6 sts on **each** of 3 needles.

Rnds 4-12: Knit around.

Rnd 13: K2 tog around: 3 sts on **each** of 3 needles for a total of 9 sts.

Rnd 14: Knit around.

Rnd 15: (K2 tog, K1) around; cut Pink leaving a long end for sewing: 2 sts on **each** of 3 needles for a total of 6 sts.

Thread yarn needle with end and slip remaining stitches onto the yarn needle; gather **tightly** and secure end.

ARM & HAND

With empty needle, pick up 2 sts at Neck edge *(Fig. J, page 8)*, slip 2 sts from st holder onto same needle, slip next 4 sts from st holder onto second empty needle, place marker around first of these 4 sts to mark beginning of rnd; slip last 2 sts from st holder onto third empty needle and with same needle, pick up 2 sts at Neck edge: 4 sts on **each** of 3 needles for a total of 12 sts.

Rnds 1-4: With Aran, knit around.

Rnd 5: K2 tog around; cut Aran: 2 sts on **each** of 3 needles for a total of 6 sts.

Rnds 6-11: With Pink, knit around; at end of Rnd 11, cut Pink leaving a long end for sewing.

Thread yarn needle with end and slip remaining stitches onto the yarn needle; gather **tightly** and secure end.

Repeat for second Arm & Hand.

SKIRT

With Head down and beginning at center of bound off stitches at back, pick up 30 sts evenly spaced across Rnd 5 of Body *(Fig. K, page 8)*, placing 10 sts onto **each** of 3 needles; place marker around first st to mark beginning of rnd.

Rnds 1-15: With Blue, knit around.

Bind off all sts in **knit**.

APRON

With Head down, pick up 8 sts centered across Rnd 1 at front of Skirt.

Row 1: With Aran, knit across.

Row 2: Purl across.

Row 3: Increase in each st across: 16 sts.

Row 4: Purl across.

Row 5: Knit across.

Rows 6-10: Repeat Rows 4 and 5 twice, then repeat Row 4 once **more**.

Row 11: K2 tog, K 12, slip 1, K1, PSSO: 14 sts.

Row 12: Purl across.

Row 13: K2 tog, K 10, slip 1, K1, PSSO: 12 sts.

Row 14: P2 tog tbl, P8, P2 tog: 10 sts.

Row 15: K2 tog across to last 2 sts, slip 1, K1, PSSO; cut Aran leaving a long end for sewing: 5 sts.

Thread yarn needle with end and slip remaining sts onto the yarn needle; do **not** gather, secure end.

EMBROIDERY (see pages 11-15)
Using photo, page 18, as a guide:

Work satin stitch using three strands of Blue floss for each eye.

Work satin stitch using three strands of Pink floss for each cheek.

Work three parallel straight stitches using three strands of Red floss for mouth, making the bottom stitch shorter than the other two.

Work scroll stitch using Aran yarn around neck, holding the Doll upside down, beginning and ending at the back.

HAIR
Cut approximately 30 strands of Yellow yarn, twice the desired finished length of hair. Attach the hair as described in Basic Hair instructions, page 15, working from the center to create a center part.

"Ahhh, this porridge is just right," she said happily and she ate it all up.

PAPA BEAR

■■■□ INTERMEDIATE

Finished Size: Approximately 9" (23 cm) tall (after felting)

MATERIALS

100% Wool Bulky Weight Yarn
[3.5 ounces, 128 yards
(100 grams, 117 meters) per skein]:
   Brown - 1 skein
90-100% Wool Medium Weight Yarn
[3.5 ounces, 220 yards
(100 grams, 201 meters) per skein]:
   Burgundy and Tweed - 1 skein **each** color
   Black - small amount for embroidery
Double pointed knitting needles, size 10½
   (6.5 mm) - set of 5 needles
Small stitch holders - 3
Split-ring marker
Yarn needle
Tapestry or embroidery needle
Gold metallic braid embroidery floss - 1 skein

The model was knit using **Cascade® 128 Chunky**
#8686 Brown, **Cascade® 220 Wool** #2412 Burgundy,
and **Cascade®** 220 Tweed #7613 Burgundy Tweed.

Techniques used:
• Increase *(Figs. 1a & b, page 80)*
• K2 tog *(Fig. 2, page 80)*
• SSK *(Figs. 7a-c, page 80)*

*Before beginning, read Basic Doll Construction,
pages 4-15.*

FIRST LEG

With Brown, cast on one st.

Row 1: (K, P, K) **all** in the same st: 3 sts.

Rows 2 and 3: Increase in each st across: 12 sts.

Row 4: Divide sts onto 3 needles as follows: K4,
(with empty needle, K4) twice: 4 sts on **each** of
3 needles.

Place marker around first st and begin working in
rnds *(see Markers, page 79)*.

Rnds 1-14: Knit around; at end of Rnd 14, cut
Brown leaving a long end for sewing.

Working counterclockwise, slip sts from each needle
onto 3 separate st holders. Leave marker to mark
third st holder.

SECOND LEG

Work same as First Leg; at end of Rnd 14, do **not**
cut Brown.

BODY

Joining Rnd: K4 from first needle; with same
needle, K4 from third st holder (front joined),
remove marker; with empty needle, K4 from
second st holder; with empty needle, K4 from last
st holder; with same needle, K4 from next needle
(back joined); with empty needle, knit last 4 sts:
8 sts on first needle, 4 sts on second needle, 8 sts on
third needle and 4 sts on fourth needle for a total of
24 sts.

Rnds 1-4: Knit around.

Begin working in rows.

Increase Row: Holding one strand **each** of Burgundy and Tweed together, K2, increase 11 times: 24 sts.

Dividing Row: Divide sts onto 4 needles as follows: P4 onto **each of** first two needles; P8 onto **each of** last 2 needles.

Hold your needles so that they form a square. With **knit** side facing, K4 from the last needle onto the first needle so that the back is joined. This needle now has 8 sts. With back facing, place marker around first st on left needle that has 4 sts. This is your new first needle.

Next 6 Rnds: Knit around; at end of last rnd, cut Burgundy and Tweed.

Increase Rnd: With Brown, increase in each st across first needle, slip sts just worked onto a st holder (Arm), move marker to first st on second needle; cut Brown, with Burgundy and Tweed, knit across 8 sts on second needle, cut Burgundy and Tweed; with Brown, increase in each st across third needle, slip sts just worked onto a second st holder (Arm), cut Brown; with Burgundy and Tweed, knit across 8 sts on last needle: 8 sts on **each** of 2 needles and 8 sts on **each** of 2 st holders for a total of 32 sts.

NECK

Rnds 1 and 2: Knit around: 8 sts on **both** needles for a total of 16 sts.

Rnd 3: K2 tog around, cut both yarns: 4 sts on **both** needles for a total of 8 sts.

Rnd 5: K8 from first needle; with same needle, K2 from second needle; with empty needle, K2 from second needle; with empty needle, K8 from third needle; with empty needle, K2 from fourth needle; slip last 2 sts from fourth needle onto first needle and remove marker: 12 sts on first needle, 2 sts on second needle, 8 sts on third needle and 2 sts on fourth needle.

Rnd 6: With empty needle, knit 12 sts from first needle; bind off remaining sts, slip last st onto first needle; cut Brown: 13 sts.

HEAD

Rnd 1: With Brown, knit around.

Rnd 2: Increase in each st around: 8 sts on **both** needles for a total of 16 sts.

Rnd 3: (K1, increase) around: 12 sts on **both** needles for a total of 24 sts.

Divide sts onto 3 needles as follows: Slip last 2 sts from second needle onto an empty needle, remove marker; with same needle, K6 from first needle; place marker around next st to mark beginning of rnd and new first needle; slip first 2 sts from second needle onto new first needle: 8 sts on **each** of 3 needles.

Rnds 4 and 5: Knit around.

MUZZLE

Rnds 1-4: Increase, knit around to last st, increase: 12 sts on first needle, 8 sts on second needle and 12 sts on third needle for a total of 32 sts.

Rnds 5-11: SSK, knit around to last 2 sts, K2 tog: 5 sts on first needle, 8 sts on second needle and 5 sts on third needle for a total of 18 sts.

Rnd 12: SSK, K3, K2 tog 4 times, K3, K2 tog: 4 sts on **each** of 3 needles for a total of 12 sts.

Rnd 13: SSK, K2 tog around; cut Brown leaving a long end for sewing: 2 sts on **each** of 3 needles for a total of 6 sts.

Thread yarn needle with end and slip remaining stitches onto the yarn needle; gather **tightly** and secure end.

ARM

With empty needle, pick up 2 sts at Neck edge *(Fig. J, page 8)*, slip 2 sts from st holder onto same needle, slip next 4 sts from st holder onto second empty needle, place marker around first of these 4 sts to mark beginning of rnd; slip last 2 sts from st holder onto third empty needle and with same needle, pick up 2 sts at Neck edge: 4 sts on **each** of 3 needles for a total of 12 sts.

Rnds 1-9: With Brown, knit around.

Rnd 10: K2 tog around; cut Brown leaving a long end for sewing: 2 sts on **each** of 3 needles for a total of 6 sts.

Thread yarn needle with end and slip remaining stitches onto the yarn needle; gather **tightly** and secure end.

Repeat for second Arm.

EAR (Make 2)

With Brown, cast on 6 sts.

Row 1: Knit across.

Row 2: Purl across.

Row 3: SSK, K2, K2 tog: 4 sts.

Row 4: Purl across.

Row 5: Knit across.

Row 6: Purl across.

Row 7: SSK, K2 tog; cut Brown leaving a long end for sewing: 2 sts.

Thread yarn needle with end and slip remaining stitches onto the yarn needle; gather **tightly** and secure end.

EMBROIDERY (see pages 11-15)
Using photo, page 22, as a guide:

Work satin stitches using Black yarn for each eye and for nose.

Work back stitch using Black yarn for mouth.

Work straight stitches using Black yarn for three claws on each paw.

Work satin stitch using Black yarn for a bow tie.

Work French knots using Black yarn for 5 buttons on his waistcoat, wrapping the yarn 4 times around the needle.

Work one straight stitch using Black yarn to make the top of a pocket.

Work back stitches using Gold braid to outline the chain of a pocket watch from one button to the pocket.

Work satin stitch using Gold braid to make the top of a watch above the pocket.

"Someone's been sleeping in my bed and she's still there!" exclaimed Baby bear.

MAMA BEAR

■■■□ **INTERMEDIATE**

Finished Size: Approximately 7" (18 cm) tall
(after felting)

MATERIALS

100% Wool Medium Weight Yarn ▣ ④
[1.75 ounces, 109 yards
(50 grams, 100 meters) per skein]:
  Brown and White - 1 skein **each** color
Double pointed knitting needles, size 8 (5 mm) -
  set of 5 needles
Small stitch holders - 3
Split-ring marker
Yarn needle
Tapestry or embroidery needle
Black and Gold embroidery floss -
  1 skein **each** color
Black pearl cotton embroidery floss #5 - 1 skein

The model was knit using **Reynolds®Lite-Lopi**
#867 Dark Brown and #51 White.

Techniques used:
- Increase *(Figs. 1a & b, page 80)*
- K2 tog *(Fig. 2, page 80)*
- P2 tog *(Fig. 4, page 80)*
- SSK *(Figs. 7a-c, page 80)*
- Slip 1, K1, PSSO *(Fig. 6, page 80)*
- P2 tog tbl *(Fig. 5, page 80)*

Before beginning, read Basic Doll Construction,
pages 4-15.

FIRST LEG

With Brown, cast on one st.

Row 1: (K, P, K) **all** in the same st: 3 sts.

Rows 2 and 3: Increase in each st across: 12 sts.

Row 4: Divide sts onto 3 needles as follows: K4,
(with empty needle, K4) twice: 4 sts on **each** of
3 needles.

Place marker around first st and begin working in
rnds *(see Markers, page 79)*.

Rnds 1-14: Knit around; at end of Rnd 14, cut
Brown leaving a long end for sewing.

Working counterclockwise, slip sts from each needle
onto 3 separate st holders. Leave marker to mark
third st holder.

SECOND LEG

Work same as First Leg; at end of Rnd 14, do **not**
cut Brown.

BODY

Joining Rnd: K4 from first needle; with same
needle, K4 from third st holder (front joined),
remove marker; with empty needle, K4 from
second st holder; with empty needle, K4 from last
st holder; with same needle, K4 from next needle
(back joined); with empty needle, knit last 4 sts:
8 sts on first needle, 4 sts on second needle, 8 sts on
third needle and 4 sts on fourth needle for a total of
24 sts.

Begin working in rows.

Increase Row: K2, increase 11 times: 24 sts.

Dividing Row: Divide sts among 4 needles as follows: P4 onto **each** of first 2 needles; P8 onto **each** of last 2 needles.

Hold your needles so that they form a square. With **knit** side facing, K4 from last needle onto first needle so that the back is joined. This needle now has 8 sts. With back facing, place marker around first st on left needle that has 4 sts. This is your new first needle.

Next 6 Rnds: Knit around.

Increase Rnd: Increase in each st across first needle, slip sts just worked onto a st holder (Arm), move marker to first st on second needle; knit across 8 sts on second needle; increase in each st across third needle, slip sts just worked onto a second st holder (Arm); knit across 8 sts on last needle: 8 sts on **each** of 2 needles and 8 sts on **each** of 2 st holders for a total of 32 sts.

NECK

Rnds 1 and 2: Knit around: 8 sts on **both** needles for a total of 16 sts.

Rnd 3: K2 tog around: 4 sts on **both** needles for a total of 8 sts.

HEAD

Rnd 1: Knit around.

Rnd 2: Increase in each st around: 8 sts on **both** needles for a total of 16 sts.

Rnd 3: (K1, increase) around: 12 sts on **both** needles for a total of 24 sts.

Rnds 1-4: Knit around.

Rnd 5: K8 from first needle; with same needle, K2 from second needle; with empty needle, K2 from second needle; with empty needle, K8 from third needle; with empty needle, K2 from fourth needle; slip last 2 sts from fourth needle onto first needle and remove marker: 12 sts on first needle, 2 sts on second needle, 8 sts on third needle and 2 sts on fourth needle.

Rnd 6: With empty needle, knit 12 sts from first needle; bind off remaining sts, slip last st onto first needle: 13 sts.

Divide sts onto 3 needles as follows: Slip last 2 sts from second needle onto an empty needle, remove marker; with same needle, K6 from first needle; place marker around next st to mark beginning of rnd and new first needle; slip first 2 sts from second needle onto first needle: 8 sts on **each** of 3 needles.

Rnds 4 and 5: Knit around.

MUZZLE
Rnds 1-4: Increase, knit around to last st, increase: 12 sts on first needle, 8 sts on second needle and 12 sts on third needle for a total of 32 sts.

Rnds 5-11: SSK, knit around to last 2 sts, K2 tog: 5 sts on first needle, 8 sts on second needle and 5 sts on third needle for a total of 18 sts.

Rnd 12: SSK, K3, K2 tog 4 times, K3, K2 tog: 4 sts on **each** of 3 needles for a total of 12 sts.

Rnd 13: SSK, K2 tog around; cut Brown leaving a long end for sewing: 2 sts on **each** of 3 needles for a total of 6 sts.

Thread yarn needle with end and slip remaining stitches onto the yarn needle; gather **tightly** and secure end.

ARM
With empty needle, pick up 2 sts at Neck edge *(Fig. J, page 8)*, slip 2 sts from st holder onto same needle, slip next 4 sts from st holder onto second empty needle, place marker around first of these 4 sts to mark beginning of rnd; slip last 2 sts from st holder onto third empty needle and with same needle, pick up 2 sts at Neck edge: 4 sts on **each** of 3 needles for a total of 12 sts.

Rnds 1-9: With Brown, knit around.

Rnd 10: K2 tog around; cut Brown leaving a long end for sewing: 2 sts on **each** of 3 needles for a total of 6 sts.

Thread yarn needle with end and slip remaining stitches onto the yarn needle; gather **tightly** and secure end.

Repeat for second Arm.

APRON
With Head down, pick up 8 sts centered across Rnd 5 on front of Body *(Fig. K, page 8)*.

Row 1: With Aran, knit across.

Row 2: Purl across.

Row 3: Increase in each st across: 16 sts.

Row 4: Purl across.

Row 5: Knit across.

Rows 6-10: Repeat Rows 4 and 5 twice, then repeat Row 4 once **more**.

Row 11: K2 tog, K 12, slip 1, K1, PSSO: 14 sts.

Row 12: Purl across.

Row 13: K2 tog, K 10, slip 1, K1, PSSO: 12 sts.

Row 14: P2 tog tbl, P8, P2 tog: 10 sts.

Row 15: K2 tog across to last 2 sts, slip 1, K1, PSSO; cut Aran leaving a long end for sewing: 5 sts.

Thread yarn needle with end and slip remaining stitches onto the yarn needle; do **not** gather, secure end.

Row 4: Purl across.

Row 5: Knit across.

Row 6: Purl across.

Row 7: SSK, K2 tog; cut Brown leaving a long end for sewing: 2 sts.

Thread yarn needle with end and slip remaining stitches onto the yarn needle; gather **tightly** and secure end.

EMBROIDERY (see pages 11-15)
Using photo, page 26, as a guide:

Work satin stitches using one strand of Black pearl cotton floss for each eye and for nose.

Work back stitch using one strand of Black pearl cotton floss for mouth.

Work straight stitches using one strand of Black pearl cotton floss for three claws on each paw.

Work split stitch using 2 strands of Gold floss to outline beehive on the apron.

Work coral stitch using 2 strands of Gold floss to make horizontal lines across the beehive.

Work straight stitches using 2 strands of Black floss to make the bees.

EAR (Make 2)
With Brown, cast on 6 sts.

Row 1: Knit across.

Row 2: Purl across.

Row 3: SSK, K2, K2 tog: 4 sts.

BABY BEAR

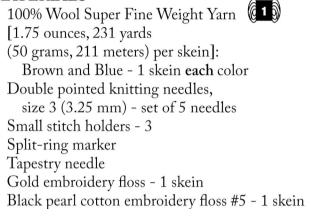

INTERMEDIATE

Finished Size: Approximately 5" (12.5 cm) tall
　　　　　　(after felting)

MATERIALS

SUPER FINE 1

　100% Wool Super Fine Weight Yarn
　[1.75 ounces, 231 yards
　(50 grams, 211 meters) per skein]:
　　Brown and Blue - 1 skein **each** color
　Double pointed knitting needles,
　　size 3 (3.25 mm) - set of 5 needles
　Small stitch holders - 3
　Split-ring marker
　Tapestry needle
　Gold embroidery floss - 1 skein
　Black pearl cotton embroidery floss #5 - 1 skein

The model was knit using **Knit Picks® Palette**
#24562 Bison and #23723 Pool.

Techniques used:
　• Increase *(Figs. 1a & b, page 80)*
　• K2 tog *(Fig. 2, page 80)*
　• SSK *(Figs. 7a-c, page 80)*

*Before beginning, read Basic Doll Construction,
pages 4-15.*

FIRST LEG

With Brown, cast on one st.

Row 1: (K, P, K) **all** in the same st: 3 sts.

Rows 2 and 3: Increase in each st across: 12 sts.

Row 4: Divide sts onto 3 needles as follows: K4,
(with empty needle, K4) twice: 4 sts on **each** of
3 needles.

Place marker around first st and begin working in
rnds *(see Markers, page 79)*.

Rnds 1-12: Knit around; at end of Rnd 12, cut
Brown.

Rnds 13 and 14: With Blue, knit around; at end of
Rnd 14; cut Blue leaving a long end for sewing.

Working counterclockwise, slip sts from each needle
onto 3 separate st holders. Leave marker to mark
third st holder.

SECOND LEG

Work same as First Leg; at end of Rnd 14, do **not**
cut Blue.

BODY

Joining Rnd: K4 from first needle; with same
needle, K4 from third st holder (front joined),
remove marker; with empty needle, K4 from
second st holder; with empty needle, K4 from last
st holder; with same needle, K4 from next needle
(back joined); with empty needle, knit last 4 sts:
8 sts on first needle, 4 sts on second needle, 8 sts on
third needle and 4 sts on fourth needle for a total of
24 sts.

Rnds 1-4: Knit around.

Rnd 5: K8 from first needle; with same needle, K2
from second needle; with empty needle, K2 from
second needle; with empty needle, K8 from third
needle; with empty needle, K2 from fourth needle;
slip last 2 sts from fourth needle onto first needle
and remove marker: 12 sts on first needle, 2 sts on
second needle, 8 sts on third needle and 2 sts on
fourth needle.

Rnd 6: With empty needle, knit 12 sts from first
needle; bind off remaining sts, slip last st onto first
needle: 13 sts.

Begin working in rows.

Increase Row: K2, increase 11 times; cut Blue: 24 sts.

Dividing Row: Divide sts among 4 needles as follows: With Brown, P4 onto **each** of first 2 needles; P8 onto **each** of last 2 needles.

Hold your needles so they form a square. With **knit** side facing, K4 from last needle onto first needle so that the back is joined. This needle now has 8 sts. With back facing, place marker around first st on left needle that has 4 sts. This is your new first needle.

Next 6 Rnds: Knit around.

Increase Rnd: Increase in each st across first needle, slip sts just worked onto a st holder (Arm), move marker to first st on second needle; knit across 8 sts on second needle; increase in each st across third needle, slip sts just worked onto a second st holder (Arm); knit across 8 sts on last needle: 8 sts on **each** of 2 needles and 8 sts on **each** of 2 st holders for a total of 32 sts.

NECK

Rnds 1 and 2: Knit around: 8 sts on **both** needles for a total of 16 sts.

Rnd 3: K2 tog around: 4 sts on **both** needles for a total of 8 sts.

HEAD

Rnd 1: Knit around.

Rnd 2: Increase in each st around: 8 sts on **both** needles for a total of 16 sts.

Rnd 3: (K1, increase) around: 12 sts on **both** needles for a total of 24 sts.

Divide sts onto 3 needles as follows: Slip last 2 sts from second needle onto an empty needle, remove marker; with same needle, K6 from first needle; place marker around next st to mark beginning of rnd and new first needle; slip first 2 sts from second needle onto first needle: 8 sts on **each** of 3 needles.

Rnds 4 and 5: Knit around.

MUZZLE

Rnds 1-4: Increase, knit around to last st, increase: 12 sts on first needle, 8 sts on second needle and 12 sts on third needle for a total of 32 sts.

Rnds 5-11: SSK, knit around to last 2 sts, K2 tog: 5 sts on first needle, 8 sts on second needle and 5 sts on third needle for a total of 18 sts.

Rnd 12: SSK, K3, K2 tog 4 times, K3, K2 tog: 4 sts on **each** of 3 needles for a total of 12 sts.

Rnd 13: SSK, K2 tog around; cut Brown leaving a long end for sewing: 2 sts on **each** of 3 needles for a total of 6 sts.

Thread tapestry needle with end and slip remaining stitches onto the tapestry needle; gather **tightly** and secure end.

ARM

With empty needle, pick up 2 sts at Neck edge *(Fig. J, page 8)*, slip 2 sts from st holder onto same needle, slip next 4 sts from st holder onto second empty needle, place marker around first of these 4 sts to mark beginning of rnd; slip last 2 sts from st holder onto third empty needle and with same needle, pick up 2 sts at Neck edge: 4 sts on **each** of 3 needles for a total of 12 sts.

Rnds 1-9: With Brown, knit around.

Rnd 10: K2 tog around; cut Brown leaving a long end for sewing: 2 sts on **each** of 3 needles for a total of 6 sts.

Thread tapestry needle with end and slip remaining stitches onto the tapestry needle; gather **tightly** and secure end.

Repeat for second Arm.

EAR (Make 2)

With Brown, cast on 6 sts.

Row 1: Knit across.

Row 2: Purl across.

Row 3: SSK, K2, K2 tog: 4 sts.

Row 4: Purl across.

Row 5: Knit across.

Row 6: Purl across.

Row 7: SSK, K2 tog; cut Brown leaving a long end for sewing: 2 sts.

Thread tapestry needle with end and slip remaining stitches onto the tapestry needle; gather **tightly** and secure end.

EMBROIDERY (see pages 11-15)

Using photo, page 30, as a guide:

Work satin stitches using one strand of Black pearl cotton floss for each eye and for nose.

Work back stitch using one strand of Black pearl cotton floss for mouth.

Work French knots using 3 strands of Gold floss to make 2 buttons on shorts, wrapping the floss around the needle 3 times.

HUMPTY-dumpty

Some people think this little rhyme is about a king who lived a long time ago. Others think it is about a large cannon placed on top of a wall just before a great battle. Because it was so large and heavy, this cannon was called "Humpty-Dumpty." During the battle, the wall came crumbling down, cannon and all. Because the cannon was so big, the king's horses and men were not able to lift it up again.

HUMPTY-DUMPTY

■■■□ INTERMEDIATE

Finished Size: Approximately 6" (15 cm) tall (after felting)

MATERIALS

100% Wool Medium Weight Yarn
[3.5 ounces, 223 yards
(100 grams, 204 meters) per skein]:
 Blue and Aran - 1 skein **each** color
 Red - small amount
Double pointed knitting needles,
 size 8 (5 mm) - set of 5 needles
Small stitch holders - 3
Split-ring marker
Yarn needle
Tapestry or embroidery needle
Black, Pink, and Red pearl cotton
 embroidery floss #5 - 1 skein **each** color

The model was knit using **Patons**® **Classic Wool** #77134 That's Blue, #00202 Aran and #00230 Bright Red.

Techniques used:

- Increase *(Figs. 1a & b, page 80)*
- K2 tog *(Fig. 2, page 80)*

Before beginning, read Basic Doll Construction, pages 4-15.

FIRST LEG

With Blue, cast on one st.

Row 1: (K, P, K) **all** in the same st: 3 sts.

Rows 2 and 3: Increase in each st across: 12 sts.

Row 4: Divide sts onto 3 needles as follows: K4, (with empty needle, K4) twice: 4 sts on **each** of 3 needles.

Place marker around first st and begin working in rnds *(see Markers, page 79)*.

Rnds 1-14: Knit around; at end of Rnd 14, cut Blue leaving a long end for sewing.

Working counterclockwise, slip sts from each needle onto 3 separate st holders. Leave marker to mark third st holder.

SECOND LEG

Work same as First Leg; at end of Rnd 14, do **not** cut Blue.

BODY

Joining Rnd: K4 from first needle; with same needle, K4 from third st holder (front joined), remove marker; with empty needle, K4 from second st holder; with empty needle, K4 from last st holder; with same needle, K4 from next needle (back joined); with empty needle, knit last 4 sts: 8 sts on first needle, 4 sts on second needle, 8 sts on third needle and 4 sts on fourth needle for a total of 24 sts.

Rnds 1-4: Knit around.

Rnd 5: K8 from first needle; with same needle, K2 from second needle; with empty needle, K2 from second needle; with empty needle, K8 from third needle; with empty needle, K2 from fourth needle; slip last 2 sts from fourth needle onto first needle and remove marker: 12 sts on first needle, 2 sts on second needle, 8 sts on third needle and 2 sts on fourth needle.

Rnd 6: With empty needle, knit 12 sts from first needle; bind off remaining sts, slip last st onto first needle: 13 sts.

Begin working in rows.

Increase Row: K1, increase, (K, P, K) **all** in each of remaining 11 sts: 36 sts.

Dividing Row: Divide sts onto 4 needles as follows: P7 onto first needle, P4 onto next needle, P 14 onto next needle, P 11 onto last needle.

Hold your needles so that they form a square. With **knit** side facing, K7 from last needle onto first needle so that back is joined. This needle now has 14 sts. With back facing, place marker around first st on left needle that has 4 sts. This is your new first needle.

Next 7 Rnds: Knit around.

Increase Rnd: Increase in each st across first needle, slip sts just worked onto a st holder (Arm), move marker to first st on second needle; knit across 14 sts on second needle; increase in each st across third needle, slip sts just worked onto a second st holder (Arm); knit across 14 sts on last needle, cut Blue: 14 sts on **each** of 2 needles and 8 sts on **each** of 2 st holders for a total of 44 sts.

HEAD

Rnds 1-6: With Aran, knit around: 14 sts on **both** needles for a total of 28 sts.

Rnd 7: ★ K2, (K2 tog, K2) 3 times; repeat from ★ once **more**: 11 sts on **both** needles for a total of 22 sts.

Rnd 8: Knit around.

Rnd 9: ★ (K2, K2 tog) twice, K3; repeat from ★ once **more**: 9 sts on **both** needles for a total of 18 sts.

Rnd 10: ★ K2 tog 4 times, K1; repeat from ★ once **more**: 5 sts on **both** needles for a total of 10 sts.

Rnd 11: ★ K2 tog twice, K1; repeat from ★ once **more**; cut Aran leaving a long end for sewing: 3 sts on **both** needles for a total of 6 sts.

Thread yarn needle with end and slip remaining stitches onto the yarn needle; gather **tightly** and secure end.

ARM & HAND

With empty needle, pick up 2 sts at Head edge *(Fig. J, page 8)*, slip 2 sts from st holder onto same needle, slip next 4 sts from st holder onto second empty needle, place marker around first of these 4 sts to mark beginning of rnd; slip last 2 sts from st holder onto third empty needle and with same needle, pick up 2 sts at Head edge: 4 sts on **each** of 3 needles for a total of 12 sts.

Rnds 1-6: With Blue, knit around; at end of Rnd 6, cut Blue.

Rnds 7-10: With Aran, knit around.

Rnd 11: K2 tog around; cut Aran leaving a long end for sewing: 2 sts on **each** of 3 needles for a total of 6 sts.

Thread yarn needle with end and slip remaining stitches onto the yarn needle; gather **tightly** and secure end.

Repeat for second Arm & Hand.

All the King's horses
And all the King's men
Couldn't put Humpty
together again!

EMBROIDERY (see pages 11-15)

Using photo, page 34, as a guide:

Work satin stitch using one strand of Black pearl cotton floss for each eye.

Work satin stitch using one strand of Pink pearl cotton floss for each cheek.

Work three parallel straight stitches using Red pearl cotton floss for mouth, making the bottom stitch shorter than the other two stitches.

Work stem stitch using Red yarn for collar.

Work French knots using Red yarn for each button, wrapping the yarn around the needle 4 times.

THE BIG bad WOLF AND THE THREE little PIGS

If you were about to build a house, would you choose to make it from straw, twigs, or bricks? The three little pigs in this story learn that planning ahead can be very important!

THE PIGS

□□□□ INTERMEDIATE

Finished Size: Approximately 5" (12.5 cm) tall (after felting)

MATERIALS

100% Wool Super Fine Weight Yarn **SUPER FINE 1**
[1.75 ounces, 231 yards
(50 grams, 211 meters) per skein]:
   Pink and Black - 1 skein **each** color
Double pointed knitting needles,
   size 3 (3.25 mm) - set of 5 needles
Small stitch holders - 3
Split-ring marker
Tapestry needle
Black, Blue and Red pearl cotton embroidery
   floss #5 - 1 skein **each** color

The models were knit using **Knit Picks® Palette** #23718 Blush and #23729 Black.

Techniques used:
- Increase *(Figs. 1a & b, page 80)*
- K2 tog *(Fig. 2, page 80)*
- SSK *(Figs. 7a-c, page 80)*

Before beginning, read Basic Doll Construction, pages 4–15.

FIRST LEG

With Black, cast on one st.

Row 1: (K, P, K) **all** in the same st: 3 sts.

Rows 2 and 3: Increase in each st across: 12 sts.

Row 4: Divide sts onto 3 needles as follows: K4, (with empty needle, K4) twice: 4 sts on **each** of 3 needles.

Place marker around first st and begin working in rnds *(see Markers, page 79)*.

Rnds 1-3: Knit around; at end of Rnd 3, cut Black.

Rnds 4-14: With Pink, knit around; at end of Rnd 14, cut Pink leaving a long end for sewing.

Working counterclockwise, slip sts from each needle onto 3 separate st holders. Leave marker to mark third st holder.

SECOND LEG

Work same as First Leg; at end of Rnd 14, do **not** cut Pink.

BODY

Joining Rnd: K4 from first needle; with same needle, K4 from third st holder (front joined), remove marker; with empty needle, K4 from second st holder; with empty needle, K4 from last st holder; with same needle, K4 from next needle (back joined); with empty needle, knit last 4 sts: 8 sts on first needle, 4 sts on second needle, 8 sts on third needle and 4 sts on fourth needle for a total of 24 sts.

Rnds 1-4: Knit around.

Rnd 5: K8 from first needle; with same needle, K2 from second needle; with empty needle, K2 from second needle; with empty needle, K8 from third needle; with empty needle, K2 from fourth needle; slip last 2 sts from fourth needle onto first needle and remove marker: 12 sts on first needle, 2 sts on second needle, 8 sts on third needle and 2 sts on fourth needle.

Rnd 6: With empty needle, knit 12 sts from first needle; bind off remaining sts, slip last st onto first needle: 13 sts.

Begin working in rows.

Increase Row: K2, increase 11 times: 24 sts.

Dividing Row: Divide sts among 4 needles as follows: P4 onto **each** of first 2 needles; P8 onto **each** of last 2 needles.

Hold your needles so that they form a square. With the **knit** side facing, K4 from last needle onto first needle so that the back is joined. This needle now has 8 sts. With back facing, place marker around first st on left needle that has 4 sts. This is your new first needle.

Next 6 Rnds: Knit around.

Increase Rnd: Increase in each st across first needle, slip sts just worked onto a st holder (Arm), move marker to first st on second needle; knit across 8 sts on second needle; increase in each st across third needle, slip sts just worked onto a second st holder (Arm); knit across 8 sts on last needle: 8 sts on **each** of 2 needles and 8 sts on **each** of 2 st holders for a total of 32 sts.

NECK

Rnds 1 and 2: Knit around: 8 sts on **both** needles for a total of 16 sts.

Rnd 3: K2 tog around: 4 sts on **both** needles for a total of 8 sts.

Rnd 4: Knit around.

HEAD

Rnd 1: Increase in each st around: 8 sts on **both** needles for a total of 16 sts.

Rnd 2: (K1, increase) around: 12 sts on **both** needles for a total of 24 sts.

Divide sts onto 3 needles as follows: Slip last 2 sts from second needle onto an empty needle, remove marker; with same needle, K6 from first needle; place marker around next st to mark beginning of rnd and new first needle; slip first 2 sts from second needle onto first needle: 8 sts on **each** of 3 needles.

Rnds 4 and 5: Knit around.

MUZZLE

Rnds 1 and 2: Increase, knit around to last st, increase: 10 sts on first needle, 8 sts on second needle, and 10 sts on third needle for a total of 28 sts.

Rnds 3-7: Knit around.

Rnd 8: SSK, knit around to last 2 sts, K2 tog: 9 sts on first needle, 8 sts on second needle and 9 sts on third needle for a total of 26 sts.

Rnd 9: SSK, knit around to last 2 sts, K2 tog: 8 sts on **each** of 3 needles for a total of 24 sts.

Rnds 10 and 11: Knit around.

Rnds 12 and 13: K2 tog around; at end of Rnd 13, cut Pink leaving a long end for sewing: 2 sts on **each** of 3 needles for a total of 6 sts.

Thread tapestry needle with end and slip remaining stitches onto the tapestry needle; gather **tightly** and secure end.

ARM

With empty needle, pick up 2 sts at Neck edge *(Fig. J, page 8)*, slip 2 sts from st holder onto same needle, slip next 4 sts from st holder onto second empty needle, place marker around first of these 4 sts to mark beginning of rnd; slip last 2 sts from st holder onto third empty needle and with same needle, pick up 2 sts at Neck edge: 4 sts on **each** of 3 needles for a total of 12 sts.

Rnds 1-6: With Pink, knit around; at end of Rnd 6, cut Pink.

Rnds 7-9: With Black, knit around.

Rnd 10: K2 tog around; cut Black leaving a long end for sewing: 2 sts on **each** of 3 needles for a total of 6 sts.

Thread tapestry needle with end and slip remaining stitches onto the tapestry needle; gather **tightly** and secure end.

Repeat for second Arm.

EAR (Make 2)

With Pink, cast on one st.

Row 1: Increase: 2 sts.

Row 2: Increase, K1: 3 sts.

Row 3: Increase, K2: 4 sts.

Row 4: K1, increase, K2: 5 sts.

Row 5: K2, increase, K2: 6 sts.

Row 6: K2 tog, K2, SSK; cut Pink leaving a long end for sewing: 4 sts.

Thread tapestry needle with end and slip remaining stitches onto the tapestry needle; gather **tightly** and secure end.

EMBROIDERY (see pages 11-15)

Using photos as a guide:

Work satin stitch using one strand of Blue pearl cotton floss for each eye.

Work back stitch using one strand of Black pearl cotton floss to outline the snout.

Work straight stitch using one strand of Black pearl cotton floss for each nostril.

Work straight stitch using one strand of Red pearl cotton floss for mouth.

THE BIG BAD WOLF

◼◼◼◻ INTERMEDIATE

Finished Size: Approximately 6½" (16.5 cm) tall (after felting and excluding Ears)

MATERIALS
100% Wool Medium Weight Yarn **4**
[3.5 ounces, 220-223 yards
(100 grams, 201-205 meters) per skein]:
  Tan, Blue, and Green - 1 skein **each** color
  Dark Brown - small amount
Double pointed knitting needles,
  size 8 (5 mm) - set of 5 needles
Small stitch holders - 3
Split-ring marker
Yarn needle
Tapestry or embroidery needle
Black and White pearl cotton embroidery
  floss #5 - 1 skein **each** color
Yellow embroidery floss - 1 skein

The model was knit using **Patons® Classic Wool** #77117 Worn Denim and #00227 Taupe and **Ella Rae Classic** #22 Taupe and #90 Kelly Green.

Techniques used:
- Increase *(Figs. 1a & b, page 80)*
- K2 tog *(Fig. 2, page 80)*
- SSK *(Figs. 7a-c, page 80)*

Before beginning, read Basic Doll Construction, pages 4-15.

FIRST LEG
With Tan, cast on one st.

Row 1: (K, P, K) **all** in the same st: 3 sts.

Rows 2 and 3: Increase in each st across: 12 sts.

Row 4: Divide sts onto 3 needles as follows: K4, (with empty needle, K4) twice: 4 sts on **each** of 3 needles.

Place marker around first st and begin working in rnds *(see Markers, page 79)*.

Rnds 1-3: Knit around; at end of Rnd 3, cut Tan.

Rnds 4-14: With Blue, knit around; at end of Rnd 14, cut Blue leaving a long end for sewing.

Working counterclockwise, slip sts from each needle onto 3 separate st holders. Leave marker to mark third st holder.

SECOND LEG
Work same as First Leg; at end of Rnd 14, do **not** cut Blue.

BODY
Joining Rnd: K4 from first needle; with same needle, K4 from third st holder (front joined), remove marker; with empty needle, K4 from second st holder; with empty needle, K4 from last st holder; with same needle, K4 from next needle (back joined); with empty needle, knit last 4 sts: 8 sts on first needle, 4 sts on second needle, 8 sts on third needle and 4 sts on fourth needle for a total of 24 sts.

Rnds 1-4: Knit around; at end of Rnd 4, cut Blue.

Rnd 5: With Dark Brown, K8 from first needle; with same needle, K2 from second needle; with empty needle, K2 from second needle; with empty needle, K8 from third needle; with empty needle, K2 from fourth needle; slip last 2 sts from fourth needle onto first needle and remove marker: 12 sts on first needle, 2 sts on second needle, 8 sts on third needle and 2 sts on fourth needle.

Rnd 6: With empty needle, knit 12 sts from first needle; bind off remaining sts, slip last st onto first needle, cut Dark Brown: 13 sts.

Begin working in rows.

Increase Row: With Green, K2, increase 11 times: 24 sts.

Dividing Row: Divide sts onto 4 needles as follows: P4 onto of **each** first 2 needles; P8 onto **each** of last 2 needles.

Hold your needles so that they form a square. With knit side facing, K4 from last needle onto first needle so that the back is joined. This needle now has 8 sts. With back facing, place marker around first st on left needle that has four sts. This is your new first needle.

Next 6 Rnds: Knit around.

Increase Rnd: Increase in each st across first needle, slip sts just worked onto a st holder (Arm), move marker to first st on second needle; knit across 8 sts on second needle; increase in each st across third needle, slip sts just worked onto a second st holder (Arm); knit across 8 sts on last needle: 8 sts on **each** of 2 needles and 8 sts on **each** of 2 st holders for a total of 32 sts.

NECK

Rnds 1 and 2: Knit around: 8 sts on **both** needles for a total of 16 sts.

Rnd 3: K2 tog around, cut Green: 4 sts on **both** needles for a total of 8 sts.

HEAD

Rnd 1: With Tan, knit around.

Rnd 2: Increase in each st around: 8 sts on **both** needles for a total of 16 sts.

Rnd 3: (K1, increase) around: 12 sts on **both** needles for a total of 24 sts.

Divide sts onto 3 needles as follows: Slip last 2 sts from second needle onto an empty needle, remove marker; with same needle, K6 from first needle; place marker around next st to mark beginning of rnd and new first needle; slip first 2 sts from second needle onto first needle: 8 sts on **each** of 3 needles.

Rnds 4 and 5: Knit around.

MUZZLE

Rnds 1-4: Increase, knit around to last st, increase: 12 sts on first needle, 8 sts on second needle and 12 sts on third needle for a total of 32 sts.

Rnds 5-11: SSK, knit around to last 2 sts, K2 tog: 5 sts on first needle, 8 sts on second needle and 5 sts on third needle for a total of 18 sts.

Rnd 12: SSK, K3, K2 tog 4 times, K3, K2 tog: 4 sts on **each** of 3 needles for a total of 12 sts.

Rnd 13: SSK, K2 tog around; cut Tan leaving a long end for sewing: 2 sts on **each** of 3 needles for a total of 6 sts.

Thread yarn needle with end and slip remaining stitches onto the yarn needle; gather **tightly** and secure end.

ARM

With empty needle, pick up 2 sts at Neck edge *(Fig. J, page 8)*, slip 2 sts from st holder onto same needle, slip next 4 sts from st holder onto second empty needle, place marker around first of these 4 sts to mark beginning of rnd; slip last 2 sts from st holder onto third empty needle and with same needle, pick up 2 sts at Neck edge: 4 sts on **each** of 3 needles for a total of 12 sts.

Rnds 1-8: With Green, knit around; at end of Rnd 8, cut Green.

Rnds 9 and 10: With Tan, knit around.

Rnd 11: K2 tog around; cut Tan leaving a long end for sewing.

Thread yarn needle with end and slip remaining stitches onto the yarn needle; gather **tightly** and secure end.

Repeat for second Arm.

EAR (Make 2)
With Tan, cast on one st.

Row 1: Knit.

Row 2: Increase: 2 sts.

Row 3: Increase, K1: 3 sts.

Row 4: P1, increase, P1: 4 sts.

Row 5: K1, increase, K2: 5 sts.

Row 6: P2, increase, P2: 6 sts.

Row 7: K2, increase, K3: 7 sts.

Row 8: P2 tog 3 times, P1: 4 sts.

Bind off all sts in **knit**.

EMBROIDERY (see pages 11-15)
Using photo, page 43, as a guide:

Work satin stitch using one strand of Black pearl cotton floss for each eye and for nose.

Work back stitch using one strand of Black pearl cotton floss to outline mouth.

Work satin stitch using one strand of White pearl cotton floss for each tooth.

Work straight stitch using one strand of Black pearl cotton floss for three claws on each paw.

Work split stitch using Dark Brown yarn to make suspenders, crossing them in the back.

Work French knots using 3 strands of Yellow floss for each button, wrapping the floss around the needle 3 times.

THE gingerbread MAN

To imagine a little gingerbread man running away through the countryside is as much fun today as it was long ago. And if you've ever eaten a cookie shaped like a gingerbread man, you know what fun it is to make one disappear!

GINGERBREAD MAN

■■■▢ INTERMEDIATE

Finished Size: Approximately 6¹/₂" (16.5 cm) tall (after felting)

MATERIALS

100% Wool Medium Weight Yarn MEDIUM 4
[3.5 ounces, 223 yards
(100 grams, 205 meters) per skein]:
   Gold - 1 skein
Double pointed knitting needles,
   size 8 (5 mm) - set of 5 needles
Small stitch holders - 3
Split-ring marker
Yarn needle
Tapestry or embroidery needle
Brown and Pink pearl cotton embroidery
   floss #5 - 1 skein **each** color
Medium Weight Yarn for embroidery - Aran

The model was knit using **Patons® Classic Wool** #00204 Old Gold and embroidered with #00202 Aran.

Techniques used:
- Increase *(Figs. 1a & b, page 80)*
- K2 tog *(Fig. 2, page 80)*

Before beginning, read Basic Doll Construction, pages 4-15.

FIRST LEG

With Gold, cast on one st.

Row 1: (K, P, K) **all** in the same st: 3 sts.

Rows 2 and 3: Increase in each st across: 12 sts.

Row 4: Divide sts onto 3 needles as follows: K4, (with empty needle, K4) twice: 4 sts on **each** of 3 needles.

Place marker around first st and begin working in rnds *(see Markers, page 79)*.

Rnds 1-14: Knit around; at end of Rnd 14, cut Gold leaving a long end for sewing.

Working counterclockwise, slip sts from each needle onto 3 separate st holders. Leave marker to mark third st holder.

SECOND LEG

Work same as First Leg; at end of Rnd 14, do **not** cut Gold.

BODY

Joining Rnd: K4 from first needle; with same needle, K4 from third st holder (front joined), remove marker; with empty needle, K4 from second st holder; with empty needle, K4 from last st holder; with same needle, K4 from next needle (back joined); with empty needle, knit last 4 sts: 8 sts on first needle, 4 sts on second needle, 8 sts on third needle and 4 sts on fourth needle for a total of 24 sts.

Rnds 1-4: Knit around.

Dividing Row: Divide sts onto 4 needles as follows: P4 onto of **each** first 2 needles; P8 onto of **each** last 2 needles.

Hold your needles so that they form a square. With **knit** side facing, K4 from last needle onto first needle so that the back is joined. This needle now has 8 sts. With back facing, place marker around first st on left needle that has 4 sts. This is your new first needle.

Next 4 Rnds: Knit around.

Increase Rnd: Increase in each st across first needle, slip sts just worked onto a st holder (Arm), move marker to first st on second needle; knit across 8 sts second needle; increase in each st across third needle, slip sts just worked onto a second st holder (Arm); knit across 8 sts on last needle: 8 sts on **each** of 2 needles and 8 sts on **each** of 2 st holders for a total of 32 sts.

NECK

Rnd 1: K2 tog around: 4 sts on **both** needles for a total of 8 sts.

Rnd 2: Knit around.

Rnd 3: Increase in each st around: 8 sts on **both** needles for a total of 16 sts.

Rnd 4: (K1, increase) around: 12 sts on **both** needles for a total of 24 sts.

Divide sts onto 3 needles as follows: Slip first 4 sts on right hand point of first needle onto an empty needle; slip first 4 sts on left hand point of second needle onto opposite end of same needle: 8 sts on **each** of 3 needles.

Rnd 5: K8 from first needle; with same needle, K2 from second needle; with empty needle, K2 from second needle; with empty needle, K8 from third needle; with empty needle, K2 from fourth needle; slip last 2 sts from fourth needle onto first needle and remove marker: 12 sts on first needle, 2 sts on second needle, 8 sts on third needle and 2 sts on fourth needle.

Rnd 6: With empty needle, knit 12 sts from first needle; bind off remaining sts, slip last st onto first needle: 13 sts.

Begin working in rows.

Increase Row: K2, increase 11 times: 24 sts.

HEAD

Rnds 1-7: Knit around.

Rnd 8: K2 tog around: 4 sts on **each** of 3 needles for a total of 12 sts.

Rnd 9: K2 tog around; cut Gold leaving a long end for sewing: 2 sts on **each** of 3 needles for a total of 6 sts.

Thread yarn needle with end and slip remaining stitches onto the yarn needle; gather **tightly** and secure end.

ARM

With empty needle, pick up 2 sts at Neck edge *(Fig. J, page 8)*, slip 2 sts from st holder onto same needle, slip next 4 sts from st holder onto second empty needle, place marker around first of these 4 sts to mark beginning of rnd; slip last 2 sts from st holder onto third empty needle and with same needle, pick up 2 sts at Neck edge: 4 sts on **each** of 3 needles for a total of 12 sts.

Rnds 1-8: With Gold, knit around.

Rnd 9: K2 tog around; cut Gold leaving a long end for sewing: 2 sts on **each** of 3 needles for a total of 6 sts.

Thread yarn needle with end and slip remaining stitches onto the yarn needle; gather **tightly** and secure end.

Repeat for second Arm.

EMBROIDERY (see pages 11-15)

Using photo, page 48, as a guide:

Work chain stitch using Aran yarn to outline the Doll in "icing."

Work satin stitch using one strand of Brown pearl cotton floss for each eye and for three buttons.

Work satin stitch using one strand of Pink pearl cotton floss for each cheek.

Work back stitch using one strand of Brown pearl cotton floss for mouth.

HANSEL and GRETEL and THE WICKED WITCH

Like the characters in many old stories, Hansel & Gretel take a fearsome and dangerous journey through the wilderness. Along the way, they can't resist the temptation of nibbling on a house made of sweet pastry and candy, not even when it is the house of a wicked witch!

HANSEL

▆▆▆▢ INTERMEDIATE

Finished Size: Approximately 6" (15 cm) tall
(after felting)

MATERIALS

100% Wool Medium Weight Yarn
[3.5 ounces, 220-223 yards
(100 grams, 201-205 meters) per skein]:
    Brown, Green, Aran, and Pink -
        1 skein **each** color
Double pointed knitting needles,
    size 8 (5 mm) - set of 5 needles
Small stitch holders - 3
Split-ring marker
Yarn needle
Tapestry or embroidery needle
Green, Purple, and Orange embroidery floss -
    1 skein **each** color
Blue, Pink, and Red pearl cotton embroidery
    floss #5 -1 skein **each** color
Super Fine Weight Yarn
    Tan for hair - small amount

The model was knit using **Patons® Classic Wool** #00231 Chestnut Brown, #77525 Moss Heather, #00202 Aran, and **Ella Rae Classic** #54 Bubblegum. His hair was made using **Knit Picks® Palette** #24242 Suede.

Techniques used:
- Increase *(Figs. 1a & b, page 80)*
- K2 tog *(Fig. 2, page 80)*

Before beginning, read Basic Doll Construction, pages 4-15.

FIRST LEG

With Brown, cast on one st.

Row 1: (K, P, K) **all** in the same st: 3 sts.

Rows 2 and 3: Increase in each st across: 12 sts.

Row 4: Divide sts onto 3 needles as follows: K4, (with empty needle, K4) twice: 4 sts on **each** of 3 needles.

Place marker around first st and begin working in rnds *(see Markers, page 79)*.

Rnds 1-3: Knit around; at end of Rnd 3, cut Brown.

Rnds 4-6: With Aran, knit around; at end of Rnd 6, cut Aran.

Rnds 7-11: With Pink, knit around; at end of Rnd 11, cut Pink.

Rnds 12 and 13: With Green, knit around; at end of Rnd 13, cut Green leaving a long end for sewing.

Working counterclockwise, slip sts from each needle onto 3 separate st holders. Leave marker to mark third st holder.

SECOND LEG

Work same as First Leg; at end of Rnd 13, do **not** cut Green.

BODY

Joining Rnd: K4 from first needle; with same needle, K4 from third st st holder (front joined), remove marker; with empty needle, K4 from second st holder; with empty needle, K4 from last st holder; with same needle, K4 from next needle (back joined); with empty needle, knit last 4 sts: 8 sts on first needle, 4 sts on second needle, 8 sts on third needle and 4 sts on fourth needle for a total of 24 sts.

Rnds 1-4: Knit around.

Hold your needles so that they form a square. With **knit** side facing, K4 from last needle onto first needle so that the back is joined; cut Brown. This needle now has 8 sts. With back facing, place marker around first st on left needle that has 4 sts. This is your new first needle.

Next 4 Rnds: With Aran, knit around.

Increase Rnd: Increase in each st across first needle, slip sts just worked onto a st holder (Arm), move marker to first st on second needle; knit across 8 sts on second needle; increase in each st across third needle, slip sts just worked onto a second st holder (Arm); knit across 8 sts on last needle: 8 sts on **each** of 2 needles and 8 sts on **each** of 2 st holders for a total of 32 sts.

NECK

Rnds 1 and 2: Knit around: 8 sts on **both** needles for a total of 16 sts.

Rnd 3: K2 tog around: 4 sts on **both** needles for a total of 8 sts.

Rnd 4: Knit around; cut Aran.

HEAD

Rnd 1: With Pink, knit around.

Rnd 2: Increase in each st around: 8 sts on **both** needles for a total of 16 sts.

Rnd 3: (K3, increase, K4) twice: 9 sts on **both** needles for a total of 18 sts.

Divide sts onto 3 needles as follows: Slip first 3 sts on right hand point of first needle onto an empty needle; slip first 3 sts on left hand point of second needle onto opposite end of same needle: 6 sts on **each** of 3 needles.

Rnds 4-12: Knit around.

Rnd 5: K8 from first needle; with same needle, K2 from second needle; with empty needle, K2 from second needle; with empty needle, K8 from third needle; with empty needle, K2 from fourth needle; slip last 2 sts from fourth needle onto first needle and remove marker: 12 sts on first needle, 2 sts on second needle, 8 sts on third needle and 2 sts on fourth needle.

Rnd 6: With empty needle, knit 12 sts from first needle; bind off remaining sts, slip last st onto first needle, cut Green: 13 sts.

Begin working in rows.

Increase Row: With Brown, K2, increase 11 times: 24 sts.

Dividing Row: Divide sts onto 4 needles as follows: P4 onto **each** of first 2 needles; P8 onto **each** of last 2 needles.

Rnd 13: K2 tog around: 3 sts on **each** of 3 needles for a total of 9 sts.

Rnd 14: Knit around.

Rnd 15: (K2 tog, K1) around; cut Pink leaving a long end for sewing: 2 sts on **each** of 3 needles for a total of 6 sts.

Thread yarn needle with end and slip remaining stitches onto the yarn needle; gather **tightly** and secure end.

ARM & HAND

With empty needle, pick up 2 sts at Neck edge *(Fig. J, page 8)*, slip 2 sts from st holder onto same needle, slip next 4 sts from st holder onto second empty needle, place marker around first of these 4 sts to mark beginning of rnd; slip last 2 sts from st holder onto third empty needle and with same needle, pick up 2 sts at Neck edge: 4 sts on **each** of 3 needles for a total of 12 sts.

Rnds 1-8: With Aran, knit around.

Rnd 9: K2 tog around: 2 sts on **each** of 3 needles for a total of 6 sts.

Rnd 10: Knit around; cut Aran.

Rnds 11-15: With Pink, knit around; at end of Rnd 15, cut Pink leaving a long end for sewing.

Thread yarn needle with end and slip remaining stitches onto the yarn needle; gather **tightly** and secure end.

Repeat for second Arm & Hand.

EMBROIDERY (see pages 11-15)

Using photo, page 52, as a guide:

Work satin stitch using one strand of Blue pearl cotton floss for each eye.

Work satin stitch using one strand of Pink pearl cotton floss for each cheek.

Work straight stitches using one strand of Red pearl cotton floss for mouth, making two stitches to form a "V" shape.

Work split stitch using 3 three strands of Green floss to make two parallel lines on each side of his shirt front for each strap, crossing the lines to form an "X" on the shirt back.

Work lazy daisy stitch using three strands of Orange or Purple floss for small flowers inside the straps.

HAIR

Use back stitches and Tan yarn to outline his face at the hairline, then make long satin stitches for the hair. Start from the center of the head and work down toward the neck. You can create parts in his hair by starting the stitching at different places.

GRETEL

⬤⬤⬤▢ INTERMEDIATE

Finished Size: Approximately 6" (15 cm) tall
(after felting)

MATERIALS

100% Wool Medium Weight Yarn ((**4**)) MEDIUM
[3.5 ounces, 220-223 yards
(100 grams, 201-205 meters) per skein]:
Brown, Green, Aran, and Pink - 1 skein
each color
Double pointed knitting needles,
size 8 (5 mm) - set of 5 needles
Small stitch holders - 3
Split-ring marker
Yarn needle
Tapestry or embroidery needle
Green, Purple, and Orange embroidery floss -
1 skein **each** color
Blue, Pink, and Red pearl cotton embroidery
floss #5 -1 skein **each** ((**1**)) SUPER FINE
Super Fine Weight Yarn
Tan for hair - small amount
Crochet hook for hair

The model was knit using **Patons® Classic Wool**
#00231 Chestnut Brown, #77525 Moss Heather,
#00202 Aran, and **Ella Rae Classic** #54 Bubblegum.
Her hair was made using **Knit Picks® Palette**
#24242 Suede.

Techniques used:
- Increase *(Figs. 1a & b, page 80)*
- K2 tog *(Fig. 2, page 80)*

*Before beginning, read Basic Doll Construction,
pages 4-8.*

FIRST LEG

With Brown, cast on one st.

Row 1: (K, P, K) all in the same st: 3 sts.

Rows 2 and 3: Increase in each st across: 12 sts.

Row 4: Divide sts onto 3 needles as follows: K4,
(with empty needle, K4) twice: 4 sts on **each** of
3 needles.

Place marker around first st and begin working in
rnds *(see Markers, page 79)*.

Rnds 1-3: Knit around; at end of Rnd 3, cut Brown.

Rnds 4-6: With Aran, knit around; at end of Rnd 6,
cut Aran.

Rnds 7-11: With Pink, knit around; at end of
Rnd 11, cut Pink.

Rnds 12 and 13: With Green, knit around; at end of
Rnd 13, cut Green leaving a long end for sewing.

Working counterclockwise, slip sts from each needle
onto 3 separate st holders. Leave marker to mark
third st holder.

SECOND LEG

Work same as First Leg; at end of Rnd 13, do **not**
cut Green.

BODY

Joining Rnd: K4 from first needle; with same
needle, K4 from third st holder (front joined),
remove marker; with empty needle, K4 from
second st holder; with empty needle, K4 from last
st holder; with same needle, K4 from next needle
(back joined); with empty needle, knit last 4 sts:
8 sts on first needle, 4 sts on second needle, 8 sts on
third needle and 4 sts on fourth needle for a total of
24 sts.

Rnds 1-4: Knit around.

Rnd 5: K8 from first needle; with same needle, K2 from second needle; with empty needle, K2 from second needle; with empty needle, K8 from third needle; with empty needle, K2 from fourth needle; slip last 2 sts from fourth needle onto first needle and remove marker: 12 sts on first needle, 2 sts on second needle, 8 sts on third needle and 2 sts on fourth needle.

Rnd 6: With empty needle, knit 12 sts from first needle; bind off remaining sts, slip last st onto first needle, cut Green: 13 sts.

Begin working in rows.

Increase Row: With Brown, K2, increase 11 times: 24 sts.

Dividing Row: Divide sts among 4 needles as follows: P4 onto **each** of first 2 needles; P8 onto **each** of last 2 needles.

Hold your needles so that they form a square. With **knit** side facing, K4 from last needle onto first needle so that the back is joined; cut Brown. This needle now has 8 sts. With back facing, place marker around first st on left needle that has 4 sts. This is your new first needle.

Next 4 Rnds: With Aran, knit around.

Increase Rnd: Increase in each st across first needle, slip sts just worked onto a st holder (Arm), move marker to first st on second needle; knit across 8 sts on second needle; increase in each st across third needle, slip sts just worked onto a second st holder (Arm); knit across 8 sts on last needle: 8 sts on **each** of 2 needles and 8 sts on **each** of 2 st holders for a total of 32 sts.

NECK

Rnds 1 and 2: Knit around: 8 sts on **both** needles for a total of 16 sts.

Rnd 3: K2 tog around: 4 sts on **both** needles for a total of 8 sts.

Rnd 4: Knit around; cut Aran.

HEAD

Rnd 1: With Pink, knit around.

Rnd 2: Increase in each st around: 8 sts on **both** needles for a total of 16 sts.

Rnd 3: (K3, increase, K4) twice: 9 sts on **both** needles for a total of 18 sts.

Divide sts onto 3 needles as follows: Slip first 3 sts on right hand point of first needle onto an empty needle; slip first 3 sts on left hand point of second needle onto opposite end of same needle: 6 sts on **each** of 3 needles.

Rnds 4-12: Knit around.

Rnd 13: K2 tog around: 3 sts on **each** of 3 needles for a total of 9 sts.

Rnd 14: Knit around.

Rnd 15: (K2 tog, K1) around; cut Pink leaving a long end for sewing: 2 sts on **each** of 3 needles for a total of 6 sts.

Thread yarn needle with end and slip remaining stitches onto the yarn needle; gather **tightly** and secure end.

ARM & HAND

With empty needle, pick up 2 sts at Neck edge *(Fig. J, page 8)*, slip 2 sts from st holder onto same needle, slip next 4 sts from st holder onto second needle, place marker around first of these 4 sts to mark beginning of rnd; slip last 2 sts from st holder onto third needle and with same needle, pick up 2 sts at Neck edge: 4 sts on **each** of 3 needles for a total of 12 sts.

Rnds 1-8: With Aran, knit around.

Rnd 9: K2 tog around: 2 sts on **each** of 3 needles for a total of 6 sts.

Rnd 10: Knit around; cut Aran.

Rnds 11-15: With Pink, knit around; at end of Rnd 15, cut Pink leaving a long end for sewing.

Thread yarn needle with end and slip remaining stitches onto the yarn needle; gather **tightly** and secure end.

Repeat for second Arm & Hand.

SKIRT

With Head down and beginning at center of bound off stitches at back, pick up 30 sts evenly spaced across Rnd 5 of Body *(Fig. K, page 8)*, placing 10 sts onto **each** of 3 needles; place marker around first st to mark beginning of rnd.

Rnds 1-10: With Green, knit around.

Bind off all sts in **knit**.

EMBROIDERY (see pages 11-15)

Using photo, page 55, as a guide:

Work satin stitch using one strand of Blue pearl cotton floss for each eye.

Work satin stitch using one strand of Pink pearl cotton floss for each cheek.

Work straight stitches using one strand of Red pearl cotton floss for mouth, making two stitches to form a "V" shape.

Work split stitch using 3 three strands of Green floss to make two parallel lines on each side of her shirt front for each strap, crossing the lines to form an "X" on the shirt back.

Work lazy daisy stitch using three strands of Orange or Purple floss for small flowers inside the straps.

HAIR

Cut approximately 30 strands of Tan yarn twice the desired finished length of hair. Attach the hair as described in Basic Hair instructions, page 15, working from the center to create a center part.

Attach several strands of yarn in same manner on her forehead for bangs. Trim close to knots.

To make the braids, gather up the strands on one side, divide into 3 groups and braid. Sew each braid to the side of her head.

Tie one strand of Purple floss in a bow around each braid.

WITCH

■■■□ INTERMEDIATE

Finished Size: Approximately 9" (23 cm) tall (after felting and including Hat)

MATERIALS

MEDIUM
4

100% Wool Medium Weight Yarn
[3.5 ounces, 220-223 yards
(100 grams, 201-205 meters) per skein]:
   Black, Green, and Purple - 1 skein **each** color
Double pointed knitting needles,
   size 8 (5 mm) - set of 5 needles
Small stitch holders - 3
Split-ring marker
Yarn needle
Tapestry or embroidery needle
Black pearl cotton embroidery floss #5 -
   1 skein
Red and Green embroidery floss -
   1 skein **each** color
Medium Weight Mohair Yarn
   White for hair - small amount
Crochet hook for hair

The model was knit using **Patons® Classic Wool** #00226 Black, #00240 Leaf Green and #77330 That's Purple. Her hair was made using Lane Borgosesia® Mohair #01 White.

Techniques used:
- Increase *(Figs. 1a & b, page 80)*
- K2 tog *(Fig. 2, page 80)*
- P2 tog *(Fig. 4, page 80)*
- P2 tog tbl *(Fig. 5, page 80)*
- SSK *(Figs. 7a-c, page 80)*

Before beginning, read Basic Doll Construction, pages 4–15.

FIRST LEG

With Black, cast on one st.

Row 1: (K, P, K) **all** in the same st: 3 sts.

Rows 2 and 3: Increase in each st across: 12 sts.

Row 4: Divide sts onto 3 needles as follows: K4, (with empty needle, K4) twice: 4 sts on **each** of 3 needles.

Place marker around first st and begin working in rnds *(see Markers, page 79)*.

Rnds 4-14: Knit around; at end of Rnd 14, cut Black leaving a long end for sewing.

Working counterclockwise, slip sts from each needle onto 3 separate st holders. Leave marker to mark third st holder.

SECOND LEG

Work same as First Leg; at end of Rnd 14, do **not** cut Black.

BODY

Joining Rnd: K4 from first needle; with same needle, K4 from third st holder (front joined), remove marker; with empty needle, K4 from second st holder; with empty needle, K4 from last st holder; with same needle, K4 from next needle (back joined); with empty needle, knit last 4 sts: 8 sts on first needle, 4 sts on second needle, 8 sts on third needle and 4 sts on fourth needle for a total of 24 sts.

Rnds 1-4: Knit around.

Rnd 5: K8 from first needle; with same needle, K2 from second needle; with empty needle, K2 from second needle; with empty needle, K8 from third needle; with empty needle, K2 from fourth needle; slip last 2 sts from fourth needle onto first needle and remove marker: 12 sts on first needle, 2 sts on second needle, 8 sts on third needle and 2 sts on fourth needle.

Rnd 6: With empty needle, knit 12 sts from first needle; bind off remaining sts, slip last st onto first needle: 13 sts.

Begin working in rows.

Increase Row: K2, increase 11 times: 24 sts.

Dividing Row: Divide sts onto 4 needles as follows: P4 onto **each** of first 2 needles; P8 onto **each** of last 2 needles.

Hold your needles so that they form a square. With **knit** side facing, K4 from last needle onto first needle so that the back is joined. This needle now has 8 sts. With back facing, place marker around first st on left needle that has 4 sts. This is your new first needle.

Next 4 Rnds: Knit around.

Increase Rnd: Increase in each st across first needle, slip sts just worked onto a st holder (Arm), move marker to first st on second needle; knit across 8 sts on second needle; increase in each st across third needle, slip sts just worked onto a second st holder (Arm); knit across 8 sts on last needle: 8 sts on **each** of 2 needles and 8 sts on **each** of 2 st holders for a total of 32 sts.

NECK
Rnds 1 and 2: Knit around: 8 sts on **both** needles for a total of 16 sts.

Rnd 3: K2 tog around: 4 sts on **both** needles for a total of 8 sts.

Rnd 4: Knit around; cut Black.

HEAD
Rnd 1: With Green, knit around.

Rnd 2: Increase in each st around: 8 sts on **both** needles for a total of 16 sts.

Rnd 3: (K3, increase, K4) twice: 9 sts on **both** needles for a total of 18 sts.

Divide sts onto 3 needles as follows: Slip first 3 sts on right hand point of first needle onto an empty needle; slip first 3 sts on left hand point of second needle onto opposite end of same needle: 6 sts on **each** of 3 needles.

Rnds 4-12: Knit around.

Rnd 13: K2 tog around: 3 sts on **each** of 3 needles for a total of 9 sts.

Rnd 14: Knit around.

Rnd 15: (K2 tog, K1) around; cut Green leaving a long end for sewing: 2 sts on **each** of 3 needles for a total of 6 sts.

Thread yarn needle with end and slip remaining stitches onto the yarn needle; gather **tightly** and secure end.

ARM & HAND
With empty needle, pick up 2 sts at neck edge *(Fig. J, page 8)*, slip 2 sts from st holder onto same needle, slip next 4 sts from st holder onto second empty needle, place marker around first of these 4 sts to mark beginning of rnd; slip last 2 sts from st holder onto third empty needle and with same needle, pick up 2 sts at Neck edge: 4 sts on **each** of 3 needles for a total of 12 sts.

Rnds 1-4: With Black, knit around.

Rnd 5: K2 tog around; cut Black: 2 sts on **each** of 3 needles for a total of 6 sts.

Rnds 6-11: With Green, knit around; at end of Rnd 11, cut Green leaving a long end for sewing.

Thread yarn needle with end and slip remaining stitches onto the yarn needle; gather **tightly** and secure end.

Repeat for second Arm and Hand.

SKIRT
With Head down and beginning at center of bound off stitches at back, pick up 30 sts evenly spaced across Rnd 5 of Body *(Fig. K, page 8)*, placing 10 sts onto **each** of 3 needles; place marker around first st to mark beginning of rnd.

Rnds 1-15: With Black, knit around; at end of Rnd 15, cut Black.

Rnd 16: With Purple, (K, P, K) **all** in each st around: 90 sts.

Rnds 17-20: Knit around.

Bind off all sts in **knit**.

BELL SLEEVE

With one Hand up and picking up sts around Rnd 5 of Arm, pick up 2 sts onto **each** of 3 needles for a total of 6 sts, place marker to mark beginning of rnd.

Rnds 1 and 2: With Black, knit around.

Rnd 3: Increase in each st around: 4 sts on **each** of 3 needles for a total of 12 sts.

Rnds 4-6: Knit around.

Rnd 7: (K, P, K) **all** in each st around: 12 sts on **each** of 3 needles for a total of 36 sts.

Bind off all sts in **knit**.

Repeat around second Arm.

BOOT TIP

With Head down and picking up sts across front of Row 4 on one Leg, pick up 6 sts.

Row 1: With Black, knit across.

Row 2: Purl across.

Row 3: K2 tog, K2, SSK: 4 sts.

Row 4: P2 tog tbl, P2 tog; cut Black leaving a long end for sewing: 2 sts.

Thread yarn needle with end and slip remaining stitches onto the yarn needle; gather **tightly** and secure end.

Repeat across second Leg.

NOSE

With front of Head facing, pick up one st in center of face.

Row 1: With Green, K1.

Row 2: P1.

Row 3: K1.

Rows 4 and 5: Repeat Rows 2 and 3; at end of Row 5, cut Green leaving a long end for sewing and pull end through st.

Thread yarn needle with end and sew top of last st to face below picked up st; secure end.

HAT

With Black, cast on 24 sts.

Divide sts placing 8 sts onto each of 3 needles and hold your needles so that they form a triangle. Place marker around first st to mark beginning of rnd.

Rnds 1-3: Knit around; at end of Rnd 3, drop Black.

Rnds 4 and 5: With Purple, knit around; at end of Rnd 5, cut Purple.

Rnd 6: With Black, (K3, K2 tog, K3) across each needle: 7 sts on **each** of 3 needles for a total of 21 sts.

Rnds 7 and 8: Knit around.

Rnd 9: (K3, K2 tog, K2) across each needle: 6 sts on **each** of 3 needles for a total of 18 sts.

Rnds 10 and 11: Knit around.

Rnd 12: (K2, K2 tog, K2) across each needle: 5 sts on **each** of 3 needles for a total of 15 sts.

Rnds 13 and 14: Knit around.

Rnd 15: (K2, K2 tog, K1) across each needle: 4 sts on **each** of 3 needles for a total of 12 sts.

Rnds 16 and 17: Knit around.

Rnd 18: (K2 tog, K2) around: 3 sts on **each** of 3 needles for a total of 9 sts.

Rnds 19 and 20: Knit around.

Rnd 21: (K2 tog, K1) around; cut Black leaving a long end for sewing: 2 sts on **each** of 3 needles for a total of 6 sts.

Thread yarn needle with end and slip remaining stitches onto the yarn needle; gather **tightly** and secure end.

BRIM

With Hat point down, using Black, picking up sts evenly spaced around cast on edge *(Fig. A)*, and beginning at joining, pick up 8 sts on **each** of 3 needles for a total of 24 sts; place marker around first st to mark beginning of rnd.

Fig. A

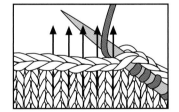

Rnd 1: Increase in each st around: 16 sts on **each** of 3 needles for a total of 48 sts.

Rnds 2-6: Knit around.

Bind off all sts in **knit**.

EMBROIDERY (see pages 11-15)

Using photo, page 58, as a guide:

Work three parallel straight stitches using three strands of Red floss for mouth, making the bottom stitch shorter than the other two.

Work a French knot using 3 strands of Green floss to make a wart on the Witch's nose.

Work satin stitch using one strand of Black pearl cotton floss for each eye.

HAIR

Cut approximately 30 strands of White mohair yarn twice the desired finished length of hair. Attach the hair as described in Basic Hair instructions, page 15, working from the center to create a center part.

RED riding HOOD AND THE wolf IN grandma's CLOTHING

Surely you would never disobey your mother or talk to a stranger! This fairytale has been told through the years to warn children about the trouble that comes from not listening to their parents. Do you think Red Riding Hood will now listen to her mother?

RED RIDING HOOD

■■■□ INTERMEDIATE

Finished Size: Approximately 7" (18 cm) tall
(after felting)

MATERIALS

100% Wool Medium Weight Yarn 【MEDIUM 4】
[3.5 ounces, 220-223 yards
(100 grams, 201-205 meters) per skein]:
Black, Aran, Pink, and Red - 1 skein
each color
Double pointed knitting needles, size 8 (5 mm) -
set of 5 needles
Straight knitting needles, size 8 (5 mm)
(for Cape only)
Small stitch holders - 3
Split-ring marker
Yarn needle
Tapestry or embroidery needle
Blue and Pink pearl cotton embroidery
floss #5 - 1 skein **each** color
Black, Green, and Red embroidery floss -
1 skein **each** color
Medium Weight Yarn
Brown for hair - small amount
Crochet hook for hair
1/8" (3 mm) wide Ribbon -
16" (40.5 cm) length

The model was knit using **Patons® Classic Wool**
#00202 Aran, #00230 Bright Red, #00226 Black,
and **Ella Rae Classic** #54 Bubblegum. Her
hair was made using Berroco® Peruvia® #7114
Chipotle.

Techniques used:
- Increase *(Figs. 1a & b, page 80)*
- K2 tog *(Fig. 2, page 80)*
- P2 tog *(Fig. 4, page 80)*
- P2 tog tbl *(Fig. 5, page 80)*
- SSK *(Figs. 7a-c, page 80)*

*Before beginning, read Basic Doll Construction,
pages 4-15.*

FIRST LEG
With Black, cast on one st.

Row 1: (K, P, K) **all** in the same st: 3 sts.

Rows 2 and 3: Increase in each st across: 12 sts.

Row 4: Divide sts onto 3 needles as follows: K4,
(with empty needle, K4) twice: 4 sts on **each** of
3 needles.

Place marker around first st and begin working in
rnds *(see Markers, page 79)*.

Rnds 1-3: Knit around; at end of Rnd 3, cut Black.

Rnds 4-14: With Aran, knit around; at end of
Rnd 14, cut Aran leaving a long end for sewing.

Working counterclockwise, slip sts from each needle
onto 3 separate st holders. Leave marker to mark
third st holder.

SECOND LEG
Work same as First Leg; at end of Rnd 14, do **not**
cut Aran.

BODY
Joining Rnd: K4 from first needle; with same
needle, K4 from third st holder (front joined),
remove marker; with empty needle, K4 from
second st holder; with empty needle, K4 from last
st holder; with same needle, K4 from next needle
(back joined); with empty needle, knit last 4 sts:
8 sts on first needle, 4 sts on second needle, 8 sts on
third needle and 4 sts on fourth needle for a total of
24 sts.

Dividing Row: Divide sts onto 4 needles as follows: P4 onto **each** of first 2 needles; P8 onto **each** of last 2 needles.

Hold your needles so that they form a square. With **knit** side facing, K4 from the last needle onto first needle so that the back is joined. This needle now has 8 sts. With back facing, place marker around first st on left needle that has 4 sts. This is your new first needle.

Next 4 Rnds: Knit around; at end of last rnd, cut Black.

Increase Rnd: With Aran, increase in each st across first needle, slip sts just worked onto a st holder (Arm), move marker to first st on second needle, cut Aran; with Black, knit across 8 sts on second needle, drop Black; with Aran, increase in each st across third needle, slip sts just worked onto a second st holder (Arm), cut Aran; with Black, knit across 8 sts on last needle: 8 sts on **each** of 2 needles and 8 sts on **each** of 2 st holders for a total of 32 sts.

NECK
Rnds 1 and 2: Knit around: 8 sts on **both** needles for a total of 16 sts.

Rnd 3: K2 tog around: 4 sts on **both** needles for a total of 8 sts.

Rnd 4: Knit around; cut Black.

HEAD
Rnd 1: With Pink, knit around.

Rnd 2: Increase in each st around: 8 sts on **both** needles for a total of 16 sts.

Rnd 3: (K3, increase, K4) twice: 9 sts on **both** needles for a total of 18 sts.

Rnds 1-4: Knit around.

Rnd 5: K8 from first needle; with same needle, K2 from second needle; with empty needle, K2 from second needle; with empty needle, K8 from third needle; with empty needle, K2 from fourth needle; slip last 2 sts from fourth needle onto first needle and remove marker: 12 sts on first needle, 2 sts on second needle, 8 sts on third needle and 2 sts on fourth needle.

Rnd 6: With empty needle, knit 12 sts from first needle; bind off remaining sts, slip last st onto first needle, cut Aran: 13 sts.

Begin working in rows.

Increase Row: With Black, K2, increase 11 times: 24 sts.

Divide sts onto 3 needles as follows: Slip first 3 sts on right hand point of first needle onto an empty needle; slip first 3 sts on left hand point of second needle onto opposite end of same needle: 6 sts on **each** of 3 needles.

Rnds 4-12: Knit around.

Rnd 13: K2 tog around: 3 sts on **each** of 3 needles for a total of 9 sts.

Rnd 14: Knit around.

Rnd 15: (K2 tog, K1) around; cut Pink leaving a long end for sewing: 2 sts on **each** of 3 needles for a total of 6 sts.

Thread yarn needle with end and slip remaining stitches onto the yarn needle; gather **tightly** and secure end.

ARM & HAND

With empty needle, pick up 2 sts at Neck edge *(Fig. J, page 8)*, slip 2 sts from st holder onto same needle, slip next 4 sts from st holder onto second needle, place marker around first of these 4 sts to mark beginning of rnd; slip last 2 sts from st holder onto third needle and with same needle, pick up 2 sts at Neck edge: 4 sts on **each** of 3 needles for a total of 12 sts.

Rnds 1-4: With Aran, knit around.

Rnd 5: K2 tog around; cut Aran: 2 sts on **each** of 3 needles for a total of 6 sts.

Rnds 6-11: With Pink, knit around; at end of Rnd 11, cut Pink leaving a long end for sewing.

Thread yarn needle with end and slip remaining stitches onto the yarn needle; gather **tightly** and secure end.

Repeat for second Arm & Hand.

SKIRT

With Head down and beginning at center of bound off stitches at back, pick up 30 sts evenly spaced across Rnd 5 of Body *(Fig. K, page 8)*, placing 10 sts onto **each** of 3 needles; place marker around first st to mark beginning of rnd.

Rnds 1-18: With Aran, knit around.

Bind off all sts in **knit**.

CAPE

With straight knitting needles and Red, cast on 51 sts.

Row 1 (Right side)**:** P2, knit across to last 2 sts, P2.

Row 2: K2, purl across to last 2 sts, K2.

Rows 3-21: Repeat Rows 1 and 2, 9 times; then repeat Row 1 once **more**.

Row 22: K2, P6, P2 tog, P5, P2 tog, P7, P2 tog twice, P6, P2 tog, P5, P2 tog, P6, K2: 45 sts.

Row 23: P2, knit across to last 2 sts, P2.

Row 24: K2, P1, (P2 tog, P1) twice, P2 tog 3 times, P1, (P2 tog, P1) 4 times, P2 tog 4 times, P1, (P2 tog, P1) twice, K2: 30 sts.

Row 25: P2, knit across to last 2 sts, P2.

Row 26: K2, P 11, P2 tog tbl, P2 tog, P 11, K2: 28 sts.

Row 27: P2, K 10, K2 tog, SSK, K 10, P2: 26 sts.

Row 28: Bind off first 2 sts in **knit**, bind off next 3 sts in **purl**, P6, P2 tog tbl, P2 tog, P8, K2: 19 sts.

Row 29: Bind off first 2 sts in **purl**, bind off next 3 sts in **knit**, knit across: 14 sts.

Row 6: K2 tog, K 18, K2 tog, SSK, K 18, K2 tog: 40 sts.

Row 7: P 18, P2 tog tbl, P2 tog, purl across: 38 sts.

Row 8: K 17, K2 tog, SSK, knit across: 36 sts.

Row 9: P 16, P2 tog tbl, P2 tog, purl across: 34 sts.

Row 10: K 15, K2 tog, SSK, knit across: 32 sts.

Row 11: P 14, P2 tog tbl, P2 tog, purl across: 30 sts.

Row 12: K2 tog 5 times, K 10, K2 tog 5 times: 20 sts.

TOP

Divide sts onto 4 needles placing 5 sts onto each needle. Hold your needles so that they form a square with the **knit** side facing. Place marker around first st to mark beginning of rnd.

Rnd 1: Knit around.

Rnd 2: (K2 tog twice, K1) around: 3 sts on **each** of 4 needles for a total of 12 sts.

Rnd 3: (K2 tog, K1) around; cut Red leaving a long end for sewing: 2 sts on **each** of 4 needles for a total of 8 sts.

Thread yarn needle with end and slip remaining stitches onto the yarn needle; gather **tightly** and secure end.

After felting, use tapestry needle to weave ribbon (like a drawstring) through the top of the Cape just under the Hood for tying Cape onto Doll.

HOOD

Row 1: Purl across.

Row 2: (K1, increase 5 times, K1) twice: 24 sts.

Row 3: Purl across.

Row 4: Increase in each st across: 48 sts.

Row 5: P2 tog, P 20, P2 tog tbl, P2 tog, P 20, P2 tog: 44 sts.

EMBROIDERY (see pages 11-15)

Using photo, page 64, as a guide:

Work satin stitch using one strand of Blue pearl cotton floss for each eye.

Work satin stitch using one strand of Pink pearl cotton floss for each cheek.

Work three parallel straight stitches using three strands of Red floss for her mouth, making the bottom stitch shorter than the other two.

Work split stitch and lazy daisy stitch using three strands of Green floss for the vine and green leaves on bodice.

Work satin stitch using three strands of Red floss for the heart.

Work split stitch and lazy daisy stitch using three strands of Red floss for the vine on the Skirt.

Work French knots using three strands of Black floss for the center of each flowers.

HAIR

Cut approximately 30 strands of Brown twice the desired finished length of hair. Attach the hair as described in Basic Hair instructions, page 15, framing her face and working all around her head.

Pull 3 strands from each side of the front to center back of head. Using photo as a guide, add French knots, wrapping floss 3 times around the needle and stem stitch with three strands of Red floss for the hair ornament.

She saw the big teeth of her grandma and asked her again, "What big teeth you have?"

THE WOLF

◼◼◼◻ INTERMEDIATE

Finished Size: Approximately 7" (18 cm) tall
(after felting and excluding cap)

MATERIALS

100% Wool Medium Weight Yarn
[3.5 ounces, 220-223 yards
(100 grams, 201-205 meters) per skein]:
   Brown, Pink, and Aran - 1 skein **each** color
Double pointed knitting needles, size 8 (5 mm) -
   set of 5 needles
Small stitch holders - 3
Split-ring marker
Yarn needle
Tapestry or embroidery needle
Black and White pearl cotton embroidery
   floss #5 - 1 skein **each** color

The model was knit using **Patons® Classic Wool**
#00202 Aran, **Ella Rae Classic** #22 Taupe and #119
Pink Heather.

Techniques used:
• Increase *(Figs. 1a & b, page 80)*
• K2 tog *(Fig. 2, page 80)*
• P2 tog *(Fig. 4, page 80)*
• SSK *(Figs. 7a-c, page 80)*

Before beginning, read Basic Doll Construction,
pages 4-15.

FIRST LEG

With Brown, cast on one st.

Row 1: (K, P, K) **all** in the same st: 3 sts.

Rows 2 and 3: Increase in each st across: 12 sts.

Row 4: Divide sts onto 3 needles as follows: K4,
(with empty needle, K4) twice: 4 sts on **each** of
3 needles.

Place marker around first st and begin working in
rnds *(see Markers, page 79)*.

Rnds 4-14: Knit around; at end of Rnd 14, cut
Brown leaving a long end for sewing.

Working counterclockwise, slip sts from each needle
onto 3 separate st holders. Leave marker to mark
third st holder.

SECOND LEG

Work same as First Leg; at end of Rnd 14, do **not**
cut Brown.

BODY

Joining Rnd: K4 from first needle; with same needle, K4 from third st holder (front joined), remove marker; with empty needle, K4 from second st holder; with empty needle, K4 from last st holder; with same needle, K4 from next needle (back joined); with empty needle, knit last 4 sts: 8 sts on first needle, 4 sts on second needle, 8 sts on third needle and 4 sts on fourth needle for a total of 24 sts.

Rnds 1-4: Knit around; at end of Rnd 4, cut Brown.

Rnd 5: With Pink, K8 from first needle; with same needle, K2 from second needle; with empty needle, K2 from second needle; with empty needle, K8 from third needle; with empty needle, K2 from fourth needle; slip last 2 sts from fourth needle onto first needle and remove marker: 12 sts on first needle, 2 sts on second needle, 8 sts on third needle and 2 sts on fourth needle.

Rnd 6: With empty needle, knit 12 sts from first needle; bind off remaining sts, slip last st onto first needle: 13 sts.

Begin working in rows.

Increase Row: K2, increase 11 times: 24 sts.

Dividing Row: Divide sts among 4 needles as follows: P4 onto **each** of first 2 needles; P8 onto **each** of last 2 needles.

Hold your needles so that they form a square. With **knit** side facing, K4 from last needle onto first needle so that the back is joined. This needle now has 8 sts. With back facing, place marker around first st on left needle that has 4 sts. This is your new first needle.

Next 4 Rnds: Knit around.

Increase Rnd: Increase in each st across first needle, slip sts just worked onto a st holder (Arm), move marker to first st on second needle; knit across 8 sts on second needle; increase in each st across third needle, slip sts just worked onto a second st holder (Arm); knit across 8 sts on last needle: 8 sts on **each** of 2 needles and 8 sts on **each** of 2 st holders for a total of 32 sts.

NECK

Rnds 1 and 2: Knit around: 8 sts on **both** needles for a total of 16 sts.

Rnd 3: K2 tog around: 4 sts on **both** needles for a total of 8 sts.

Rnd 4: Knit around; cut Pink.

HEAD

Rnd 1: With Brown, increase in each st around: 8 sts on **both** needles for a total of 16 sts.

Rnd 2: (K1, increase) around: 12 sts on **both** needles for a total of 24 sts.

Divide sts onto 3 needles as follows: Slip last 2 sts from second needle onto an empty needle, remove marker; with same needle, K6 from first needle; place marker around next st to mark beginning of rnd and new first needle; slip first 2 sts from second needle onto first needle: 8 sts on **each** of 3 needles.

Rnds 4 and 5: Knit around.

MUZZLE

Rnds 1-4: Increase, knit around to last st, increase: 12 sts on first needle, 8 sts on second needle and 12 sts on third needle for a total of 32 sts.

Rnds 5-11: SSK, knit around to last 2 sts, K2 tog: 5 sts on first needle, 8 sts on second needle and 5 sts on third needle for a total of 18 sts.

Rnd 12: SSK, K3, K2 tog 4 times, K3, K2 tog: 4 sts on **each** of 3 needles for a total of 12 sts.

Rnd 13: SSK, K2 tog around; cut Brown leaving a long end for sewing: 2 sts on **each** of 3 needles for a total of 6 sts.

Thread yarn needle with end and slip remaining stitches onto the yarn needle; gather **tightly** and secure end.

ARM

With empty needle, pick up 2 sts at Neck edge *(Fig. J, page 8)*, slip 2 sts from st holder onto same needle, slip next 4 sts from st holder onto second needle, place marker around first of these 4 sts to mark beginning of rnd; slip last 2 sts from st holder onto third needle and with same needle, pick up 2 sts at Neck edge: 4 sts on **each** of 3 needles for a total of 12 sts.

Rnds 1-7: With Pink, knit around; at end of Rnd 7, cut Pink.

Rnds 8 and 9: With Brown, knit around.

Rnd 10: K2 tog around; cut Brown leaving a long end for sewing: 2 sts on **each** of 3 needles for a total of 6 sts.

Thread yarn needle with end and slip remaining stitches onto the yarn needle; gather **tightly** and secure end.

Repeat for second Arm.

SKIRT

With Head down and beginning at center of bound off stitches at back, pick up 30 sts evenly spaced across Rnd 5 of Body *(Fig. K, page 8)*, placing 10 sts onto **each** of 3 needles; place marker around first st to mark beginning of rnd.

Rnds 1-15: With Pink, knit around.

Bind off all sts in **knit**.

EAR (Make 2)

With Brown, cast on one st.

Row 1: K1.

Row 2: Increase: 2 sts.

Row 3: Increase, K1: 3 sts.

Row 4: P1, increase, P1: 4 sts.

Row 5: K1, increase, K2: 5 sts.

Row 6: P2, increase, P2: 6 sts.

Row 7: K2, increase, K3: 7 sts.

Row 8: P2 tog 3 times, P1: 4 sts.

Bind off remaining sts in **knit**.

MOB CAP

With Aran, cast on one st.

Row 1: (K, P, K) **all** in the same st: 3 sts.

Rows 2 and 3: Increase in each st across: 12 sts.

Row 4: Divide sts onto 3 needles as follows: K4, (with empty needle, K4) twice: 4 sts on **each** of 3 needles.

Place marker around first st and begin working in rnds.

Rnd 1: Increase in each st around: 8 sts on **each** of 3 needles for a total of 24 sts.

Rnd 2: (K1, increase) around: 12 sts on **each** of 3 needles for a total of 36 sts.

Rnds 3-7: Knit around.

Rnd 8: (K, P, K) **all** in each st around: 36 sts on **each** of 3 needles for a total of 108 sts.

Rnds 9 and 10: Knit around.

Bind off all sts in **knit**.

After the Cap is felted, thread yarn needle with a long strand of Pink yarn and weave the strand like a drawstring through stitches on Rnd 6. Tie the ends in a bow.

EMBROIDERY (see pages 11-15)
Using photo, page 68, as a guide:

Work satin stitch using one strand of Black pearl cotton floss for each eye and the nose.

Work back stitch using one strand of Black pearl cotton floss to outline the spectacles right under the eyes.

Work back stitch using one strand of Black pearl cotton floss to outline the mouth.

Work satin stitch using one strand of White pearl cotton floss for the teeth.

Work straight stitch using one strand of Black pearl cotton floss for the claws.

Work chain stitch using one strand of White pearl cotton floss for collar and cuffs.

Work French knots using one strand of White pearl cotton floss for buttons, wrapping the floss 3 times around the needle.

MARY and her little LAMB

This sweet nursery rhyme is so beloved it has also become a popular children's song. But did you know it is a true story? Mary Sawyer was a little girl who lived in New England almost two hundred years ago. She really did take her pet lamb to school one day. There was young man there who thought it was amusing to see a lamb in school. He wrote the first three verses of the famous rhyme and gave them to Mary as a gift.

MARY

■■■□ INTERMEDIATE

Finished Size: Approximately 6½" (16.5 cm) tall (after felting)

MATERIALS

100% Wool Medium Weight Yarn 【4】
[3.5 ounces, 220-223 yards
(100 grams, 201-205 meters) per skein]:
   Black, Aran, Burgundy, and Pink -
    1 skein **each** color
Double pointed knitting needles, size 8 (5 mm) -
   set of 5 needles
Small stitch holders - 3
Split-ring marker
Yarn needle
Tapestry or embroidery needle
Black and Red pearl cotton embroidery
   floss #5 - 1 skein **each** color
Medium Weight Yarn
   Brown for hair - small amount
Crochet hook for hair

The model was knit with **Patons Classic Wool**
#00202 Aran, and **Ella Rae Classic** #62 Burgundy,
#32 Black and #54 Bubblegum. Her hair was made
using **Lion Wool** #125 Cocoa.

Techniques used:
- Increase *(Figs. 1a & b, page 80)*
- K2 tog *(Fig. 2, page 80)*
- K3 tog *(Fig. 3, page 80)*

Before beginning, read Basic Doll Construction, pages 4-15.

FIRST LEG

With Black, cast on one st.

Row 1: (K, P, K) **all** in the same st: 3 sts.

Rows 2 and 3: Increase in each st across: 12 sts.

Row 4: Divide sts onto 3 needles as follows: K4, (with empty needle, K4) twice: 4 sts on **each** of 3 needles.

Place marker around first st and begin working in rnds *(see Markers, page 79)*.

Rnds 1-3: Knit around; at end of Rnd 3, cut Black.

Rnds 4-14: With Aran, knit around; at end of Rnd 14, cut aran leaving a long end for sewing.

Working counterclockwise, slip sts from each needle onto 3 separate st holders. Leave marker to mark third st holder.

SECOND LEG

Work same as First Leg; at end of Rnd 14, do **not** cut Aran.

BODY

Joining Rnd: K4 from first needle; with same needle, K4 from third st holder (front joined), remove marker; with empty needle, K4 from second st holder; with empty needle, K4 from last st holder; with same needle, K4 from next needle (back joined); with empty needle, knit last 4 sts: 8 sts on first needle, 4 sts on second needle, 8 sts on third needle and 4 sts on fourth needle for a total of 24 sts.

Rnds 1-4: Knit around; at end of Rnd 4, cut Aran.

Rnd 5: With Burgundy, K8 from first needle; with same needle, K2 from second needle; with empty needle, K2 from second needle; with empty needle, K8 from third needle; with empty needle, K2 from fourth needle; slip last 2 sts from fourth needle onto first needle and remove marker: 12 sts on first needle, 2 sts on second needle, 8 sts on third needle and 2 sts on fourth needle.

Rnd 6: With empty needle, knit 12 sts from first needle; bind off remaining sts, slip last st onto first needle: 13 sts.

Begin working in rows.

Increase Row: K2, increase 11 times: 24 sts.

Dividing Row: Divide sts onto 4 needles as follows: P4 onto **each** of first 2 needles; P8 onto **each** of last 2 needles.

Hold your needles so that they form a square. With the **knit** side facing, K4 from last needle onto first needle so that the back is joined. This needle now has 8 sts. With back facing, place marker around first st on left needle that has 4 sts. This is your new first needle.

Next 4 Rnds: Knit around.

Increase Rnd: Increase in each st across first needle, slip sts just worked onto a st holder (Arm), move marker to first st on second needle; knit across 8 sts on second needle; increase in each st across third needle, slip sts just worked onto a second st holder (Arm); knit across 8 sts on last needle: 8 sts on **each** of 2 needles and 8 sts on **each** of 2 st holders for a total of 32 sts.

NECK

Rnds 1 and 2: Knit around: 8 sts on **both** needles for a total of 16 sts.

Rnd 3: K2 tog around: 4 sts on **both** needles for a total of 8 sts.

Rnd 4: Knit around; cut Burgundy.

HEAD

Rnd 1: With Pink, knit around.

Rnd 2: Increase in each st around: 8 sts on **both** needles for a total of 16 sts.

Rnd 3: (K3, increase, K4) across each needle: 9 sts on **both** needles for a total of 18 sts.

Divide sts onto 3 needles as follows: Slip first 3 sts on right hand point of first needle onto an empty needle; slip first 3 sts on left hand point of second needle onto opposite end of same needle: 6 sts on **each** of 3 needles.

Rnds 4-12: Knit around.

Rnd 13: K2 tog around: 3 sts on **each** of 3 needles for a total of 9 sts.

Rnd 14: Knit around.

Rnd 15: (K2 tog, K1) around; cut Pink leaving a long end for sewing: 2 sts on **each** of 3 needles for a total of 6 sts.

Thread yarn needle with end and slip remaining stitches onto the yarn needle; gather **tightly** and secure end.

ARM & HAND

With empty needle, pick up 2 sts at Neck edge *(Fig. J, page 8)*, slip 2 sts from st holder onto same needle, slip next 4 sts from st holder onto second needle, place marker around first of these 4 sts to mark beginning of rnd; slip last 2 sts from st holder onto third needle and with same needle, pick up 2 sts at Neck edge: 4 sts on **each** of 3 needles for a total of 12 sts.

Rnds 1-6: With Burgundy, knit around.

Rnd 7: K2 tog around; cut Burgundy: 2 sts on **each** of 3 needles for a total of 6 sts.

Rnds 8-11: With Pink, knit around; at end of Rnd 11, cut Pink leaving a long end for sewing.

Thread yarn needle with end and slip remaining stitches onto the yarn needle; gather **tightly** and secure end.

Repeat for second Arm & Hand.

SKIRT

With Head down and beginning at center of bound off stitches at back, pick up 30 sts evenly spaced across Rnd 5 of Body *(Fig. K, page 8)*, placing 10 sts onto **each** of 3 needles; place marker around first st to mark beginning of rnd.

Rnds 1-10: With Burgundy, knit around.

Rnd 11: (K, P, K) **all** in each st around: 90 sts.

Rnds 12 and 13: Knit around.

Rnd 14: K3 tog around: 30 sts.

Bind off all sts in **knit**.

EMBROIDERY (see pages 11-15)

Using photo, page 74, as a guide:

Work satin stitches using one strand of Black pearl cotton floss for each eye.

Work parallel straight stitches using one strand of Red pearl cotton floss for mouth, making bottom stitch shorter than the top one.

Use chain stitch using Aran yarn around the Neck Work the collar and around each hand for cuffs.

Work French knots using Aran yarn for 2 buttons, wrapping the yarn 4 times around the needle.

HAIR

Cut approximately 30 strands of Brown yarn twice the desired finished length of hair. Attach the hair as described in Basic Hair instructions, page 15, framing her face and working all around her head.

Gather the long strands up into a ponytail, tying a piece of Brown around it to secure. Stitch through the yarn and into the hair to hold the ponytail in place. Wrap a strand of Burgundy yarn around the ponytail, tying into a bow. Stitch in place to secure.

LAMB

◼◼◼◻ INTERMEDIATE

Finished Size: Approximately 5" (12.5 cm) tall (after felting)

MATERIALS

100% Wool Super Fine Weight Yarn
[1.75 ounces, 231 yards
(50 grams, 211 meters) per skein]:
Cream and Black - 1 skein **each** color
100% Nylon Light Weight Novelty Yarn
[1.75 ounces, 140 yards
(50 grams, 128 meters) per skein]:
White - 1 skein
Double pointed knitting needles,
size 3 (3.25 mm) - set of 5 needles
Small stitch holders - 3
Split-ring marker
Yarn needle
Tapestry or embroidery needle
Black pearl cotton embroidery floss #5 - 1 skein

The model was knit with **Knit Picks® Palette** #23730 Cream and **Sirdar® Snuggly Bubbly** #190 White.

Techniques used:
• Increase *(Figs. 1a & b, page 80)*
• K2 tog *(Fig. 2, page 80)*
• SSK *(Figs. 7a-c, page 80)*

Before beginning, read Basic Doll Construction, pages 4-15.

FIRST LEG

With Black, cast on one st.

Row 1: (K, P, K) **all** in the same st: 3 sts.

Rows 2 and 3: Increase in each st across: 12 sts.

Row 4: Divide sts onto 3 needles as follows: K4, (with empty needle, K4) twice: 4 sts on **each** of 3 needles.

Place marker around first st and begin working in rnds *(see Markers, page 79)*.

Rnds 1-3: Knit around; at end of Rnd 3, cut Black.

Rnds 4-10: With Cream, knit around.

Rnds 11-14: With one strand **each** of Cream and White, knit around; at end of Rnd 14, cut both yarns leaving a long end of Cream for sewing.

Working counterclockwise, slip sts from each needle onto 3 separate st holders. Leave marker to mark third st holder.

SECOND LEG

Work same as First Leg; at end of Rnd 14, do **not** cut yarns.

BODY

Joining Rnd: K4 from first needle; with same needle, K4 from third st holder (front joined), remove marker; with empty needle, K4 from second st holder; with empty needle, K4 from last st holder; with same needle, K4 from next needle (back joined); with empty needle, knit last 4 sts: 8 sts on first needle, 4 sts on second needle, 8 sts on third needle and 4 sts on fourth needle for a total of 24 sts.

Rnds 1-4: Knit around.

Rnd 5: K8 from first needle; with same needle, K2 from second needle; with empty needle, K2 from second needle; with empty needle, K8 from third needle; with empty needle, K2 from fourth needle; slip last 2 sts from fourth needle onto first needle and remove marker: 12 sts on first needle, 2 sts on second needle, 8 sts on third needle and 2 sts on fourth needle.

Rnd 6: With empty needle, knit 12 sts from first needle; bind off remaining sts, slip last st onto first needle.

Begin working in rows.

Increase Row: K2, increase 11 times: 24 sts.

Dividing Row: Divide sts among 4 needles as follows: P4 onto **each** of first 2 needles; P8 onto **each** of last 2 needles.

Hold your needles so that they form a square. With **knit** side facing, K4 from last needle onto first needle so the back is joined. This needle now has 8 sts. With back facing, place marker around first st on left needle that has 4 sts. This is your new first needle.

Next 6 Rnds: Knit around.

Increase Rnd: Increase in each st across first needle, slip sts just worked onto a st holder (Arm), move marker to first st on second needle; knit across 8 sts on second needle; increase in each st across third needle, slip sts just worked onto a second st holder (Arm); knit across 8 sts on last needle: 8 sts on **each** of 2 needles and 8 sts on **each** of 2 st holders for a total of 32 sts.

NECK
Rnds 1 and 2: Knit around: 8 sts on **both** needles for a total of 16 sts.

Rnd 3: K2 tog around: 4 sts on **both** needles for a total of 8 sts.

Rnd 4: Knit around.

HEAD
Rnd 1: Increase in each st around: 8 sts on **both** needles for a total of 16 sts.

Rnd 2: (K1, increase) around: 12 sts on **both** needles for a total of 24 sts.

Divide sts onto 3 needles as follows: Slip last 2 sts from second needle onto an empty needle, remove marker; with same needle, K6 from first needle; place marker around next st to mark beginning of rnd and new first needle; slip first 2 sts from second needle onto first needle: 8 sts on **each** of 3 needles.

Rnds 4 and 5: Knit around; at end of Rnd 5, cut White only.

MUZZLE

Rnds 1 and 2: Increase, knit around to last st, increase: 10 sts on first needle, 8 sts on second needle, and 10 sts on third needle for a total of 28 sts.

Rnds 3-7: Knit around.

Rnd 8: SSK, knit around to last 2 sts, K2 tog: 26 sts.

Rnd 9: SSK, knit around to last 2 sts, K2 tog: 24 sts.

Rnds 10 and 11: Knit around.

Rnds 12 and 13: With one strand **each** of Cream and White, K2 tog around; at end of Rnd 13, cut both yarns leaving long ends for sewing: 2 sts on **each** needle for a total of 6 sts.

Thread yarn needle with ends and slip remaining stitches onto the yarn needle; gather **tightly** and secure ends.

ARM

With empty needle, pick up 2 sts at Neck edge *(Fig. J, page 8)*, slip 2 sts from st holder onto same needle, slip next 4 sts from st holder onto second needle, place marker around first of these 4 sts to mark beginning of rnd; slip last 2 sts from st holder onto third needle and with same needle, pick up 2 sts at Neck edge: 4 sts on **each** of 3 needles for a total of 12 sts.

Rnds 1-6: With Cream, knit around; at end of Rnd 6, cut Cream.

Rnds 7-9: With Black, knit around.

Rnd 10: K2 tog around; cut Black leaving a long end for sewing: 2 sts on **each** of 3 needles for a total of 6 sts.

Thread yarn needle with end and slip remaining stitches onto the yarn needle; gather **tightly** and secure end.

Repeat for second Arm.

EAR (Make 2)

With Cream, cast on one st.

Row 1: Increase: 2 sts.

Row 2: Increase, K1: 3 sts.

Row 3: Increase, K2: 4 sts.

Row 4: K1, increase, K2: 5 sts.

Row 5: K2, increase, K2: 6 sts.

Row 6: K2 tog, K2, SSK; cut Cream leaving a long end for sewing: 4 sts.

Thread yarn needle with end and slip remaining stitches onto the yarn needle; gather **tightly** and secure end.

EMBROIDERY (see pages 11-15)

Using photo, page 77, as a guide:

Work satin stitch using one strand of Black pearl cotton floss for each eye.

Work two parellel straight stitches using one strand of Black pearl cotton floss for mouth. Work a third stitch, starting just under the middle of the bottom stitch, going up and around the top stitch, pulling the two stitches close to each other, forming an "X" shape.

general INSTRUCTIONS

ABBREVIATIONS

cm	centimeters
K	knit
mm	millimeters
P	purl
PSSO	pass slipped stitch over
Rnd(s)	Round(s)
SSK	slip, slip, knit
st(s)	stitch(es)
tbl	through back loop(s)
tog	together

★ — work instructions following ★ as many **more** times as indicated in addition to the first time.

( ) or [ ] — work enclosed instructions **as many** times as specified by the number immediately following **or** work all enclosed instructions in the stitch indicated **or** contains explanatory remarks.

colon (:) — the number(s) given after a colon at the end of a row or round denote(s) the number of stitches you should have on that row or round.

MARKERS

As a convenience to you, we have used markers to help distinguish the beginning of a pattern or a round. Place markers as instructed. When you reach a marker on each row or round, slip it onto the first st; remove it when no longer needed.

KNIT TERMINOLOGY

UNITED STATES	INTERNATIONAL
gauge =	tension
bind off =	cast off
yarn over (YO) =	yarn forward (yfwd) **or** yarn around needle (yrn)

Yarn Weight Symbol & Names	LACE 0	SUPER FINE 1	FINE 2	LIGHT 3	MEDIUM 4	BULKY 5	SUPER BULKY 6
Type of Yarns in Category	Fingering, size 10 crochet thread	Sock, Fingering, Baby	Sport, Baby	DK, Light Worsted	Worsted, Afghan, Aran	Chunky, Craft, Rug	Bulky, Roving
Knit Gauge Range* in Stockinette St to 4" (10 cm)	33-40** sts	27-32 sts	23-26 sts	21-24 sts	16-20 sts	12-15 sts	6-11 sts
Advised Needle Size Range	000-1	1 to 3	3 to 5	5 to 7	7 to 9	9 to 11	11 and larger

*GUIDELINES ONLY: The chart above reflects the most commonly used gauges and needle sizes for specific yarn categories.

** Lace weight yarns are usually knitted on larger needles to create lacy openwork patterns. Accordingly, a gauge range is difficult to determine. Always follow the gauge stated in your pattern.

KNITTING NEEDLES															
U.S.	0	1	2	3	4	5	6	7	8	9	10	10½	11	13	15	17
U.K.	13	12	11	10	9	8	7	6	5	4	3	2	1	00	000	---
Metric - mm	2	2.25	2.75	3.25	3.5	3.75	4	4.5	5	5.5	6	6.5	8	9	10	12.75

●■□□□ BEGINNER	Projects for first-time knitters using basic knit and purl stitches. Minimal shaping.
●■■□□ EASY	Projects using basic stitches, repetitive stitch patterns, simple color changes, and simple shaping and finishing.
●■■■□ INTERMEDIATE	Projects with a variety of stitches, such as basic cables and lace, simple intarsia, double-pointed needles and knitting in the round needle techniques, mid-level shaping and finishing.
●■■■■ EXPERIENCED	Projects using advanced techniques and stitches, such as short rows, fair isle, more intricate intarsia, cables, lace patterns, and numerous color changes.

INCREASE

Knit the next stitch but do **not** slip the old stitch off the left needle *(Fig. 1a)*. Insert the right needle into the **back** loop of the **same** stitch and knit it *(Fig. 1b)*, then slip the old stitch off the left needle.

Fig. 1a

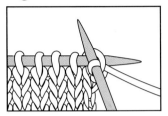

Fig. 1b

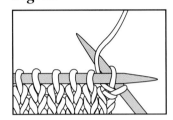

DECREASES
KNIT 2 TOGETHER
(abbreviated K2 tog)
Insert the right needle into the **front** of the first two stitches on the left needle as if to **knit** *(Fig. 2)*, then **knit** them together as if they were one stitch.

Fig. 2

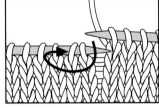

KNIT 3 TOGETHER
(abbreviated K3 tog)
Insert the right needle into the **front** of the first three stitches on the left needle as if to **knit** *(Fig. 3)*, then **knit** them together as if they were one stitch.

Fig. 3

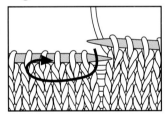

PURL 2 TOGETHER
(abbreviated P2 tog)
Insert the right needle into the **front** of the first two stitches on the left needle as if to **purl** *(Fig. 4)*, then **purl** them together as if they were one stitch.

Fig. 4

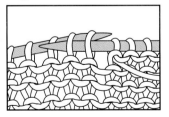

PURL 2 TOGETHER THROUGH THE BACK LOOP
(abbreviated P2 tog tbl)
Insert the right needle into the **back** of both stitches from **back** to **front** *(Fig. 5)*, then **purl** them together as if they were one stitch.

Fig. 5

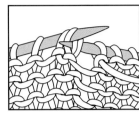

SLIP 1, KNIT 1, PASS SLIPPED STITCH OVER
(abbreviated slip 1, K1, PSSO)
Slip one stitch as if to **knit**. Knit the next stitch. With the left needle, bring the slipped stitch over the knit stitch *(Fig. 6)* and off the needle.

Fig. 6

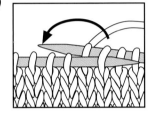

SLIP, SLIP, KNIT
(abbreviated SSK)
Separately slip two stitches as if to **knit** *(Fig. 7a)*. Insert the left needle into the **front** of both slipped stitches *(Fig. 7b)* and knit them together as if they were one stitch *(Fig. 7c)* .

Fig. 7a

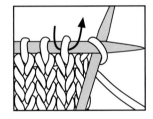

Fig. 7b

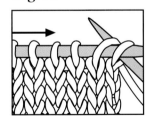

Fig. 7c

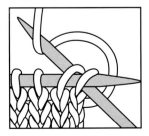